DIGNIFIED HEDONISM

A collection of
BASIC INSTRUCTIONS
by Scott Meyer

basicinstructions.net

So here we are again, at the introduction page of one of my collections of Basic Instructions comics. If you've read any of my three earlier collections, then you'll have already noticed that this one seems different somehow. It's not your imagination. It is different in three key ways.

1.   It is larger. This allows me to print the comics at a larger size, which in turn allows you, the reader, to more fully appreciate the beauty and grandeur of the same five or six drawings I use over and over again.

2.   The pages are white. To those who did not see my previous books this might seem like an odd thing to point out. Counter-intuitive as it may seem, all three of my earlier collections featured the individual comics embedded in a uniform field of black. This made for a bold, unique design. For this collection I have instead gone with white pages, on which the comics are displayed in the same layout as when they originally appeared on basicinstructions.net. I made this change because it will make life easier for future scholars, and it is much less work for me.

3.   It is all comics. The last pages of earlier books contained "bonus materials." Aside from occasional commentaries, this book has no bonus materials. Instead, I have filled that space with more Basic Instructions comics. You are free to consider that a "bonus" if you wish.

I feel very fortunate to get to make my comic, and I am grateful to those who have made it possible. As you seem to be someone who has somehow procured a copy of this book, logically, that includes you.

Most of us spend our lives bound by rules and social conventions. In order to stay sane we must occasionally cut loose.

We could eat hot wings or play Monopoly.

Or we could wallow in unbridled hedonism!

Must it be "unbridled"?

We could wallow in reserved, dignified hedonism, but what's the point?

What form your hedonism will take is personal, and will be determined by your needs, desires, and particular tastes.

Hedonism sounds good in theory, but what would we actually do?

Anything, as long as we do it with gusto, and no thought to the consequences.

So it's all about attitude.

You're over-thinking this.

Yes, but with gusto!

If you do wallow in unbridled hedonism, do it right. Banish thoughts of propriety. Forget consequences. Live in the now.

I've got wing sauce all over my face, and it feels great!

And painful.

I'm buying Baltic Avenue BABY, and I don't care who knows it!

Note: Disregarding consequences doesn't mean there won't be any, or that you won't have regrets later.

My taste buds all fell off and my face is stained, maybe permanently.

I have all that, plus my Monopoly set is ruined.

We're wallowing in unbridled remorse.

You know it, baby!

basicinstructions.net

This comic is a bit unrealistic. Nobody will play Monopoly with me, not even my wife. It's partially because the last time we played I beat her in less than thirty minutes, and partly because I've told that story too many times.

How to Tell a Scary Story

by Scott MEYER

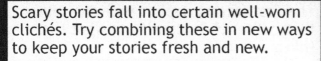

Panel 1:

Scary stories fall into certain well-worn clichés. Try combining these in new ways to keep your stories fresh and new.

The boy would have to spend the night in a graveyard. A graveyard built on an ancient Indian burial ground.

How'd they build a graveyard on a burial ground?

It was a shallow graveyard, for the bereaved but budget-conscious.

Panel 2:

Since these clichés have been around forever, they are inherently outdated. You will need to adapt them for today.

I think you should call it a Native American burial ground.

No, I shouldn't, because these Indians are actual people from India.

And I'll thank you not to interrupt me with your outdated, racist assumptions.

Panel 3:

Layer on plenty of detail. This will make your story more vivid and relatable.

They had sailed east from Visakhapatnam. They'd hoped to find a trading route to Spain. They hit North America instead.

Good thing too! If North America hadn't been there they would have eventually had a head-on collision with Columbus!

Panel 4:

Remember that the details serve the plot. Don't let them overshadow the primary plot of your story.

The voice said "My name is Goooooptaaaaa!"

In India, don't they cremate their dead?

Uh, yeah. That's why the ghosts are angry.

But then why

Look, you wanna hear this story, or do you wanna ask questions?

If they all died, who buried them?

basicinstructions.net

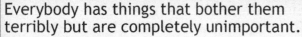

BASIC INSTRUCTIONS

How to Deal with the Little Things That Really Bother You

by Scott MEYER

Panel 1:

Everybody has things that bother them terribly but are completely unimportant.

Do you have any pet peeves?

Yes. I can't stand the phrase "pet peeve."

Wow, that's pretty "meta."

Yeah, don't like "meta" much either.

Panel 2:

The first step to dealing with the things that bother us is identifying what those things are in the first place.

What else do you hate?

I don't "hate." Hatred is useless and destructive.

You hate John Cougar Mellencamp.

No, I loathe John Cougar Mellencamp. There's a big difference.

Panel 3:

Once you've identified what's bothering you, try to determine why it bothers you.

He leaves his small town, goes to New York, changes his name to "Johnny Cougar" and records pop songs. Once he's famous he changes his name back and squirts out songs about how great small towns are and how he doesn't wanna be a pop singer.

Isn't there anything you like about him?

I don't want him to be a pop singer either, so we have some common ground there.

Panel 4:

Now prove to yourself that it's useless getting angry about it. You'll still get angry. You'll just know it's silly.

It's funny. You've put all this energy into disliking John Mellencamp, and he has no idea that you even exist.

I don't find that funny.

I bet he would.

© 2010: Scott Meyer

Did you know Adobe's spell checker

basicinstructions.net

This comic expresses my genuine emotions about John Cougar Mellencamp. If we're in public and one of his "songs" comes on, poor Missy gets to hear me recite panel three in its entirety. I also resent his hair, because he has so much of it and he seems to style it with motor oil.

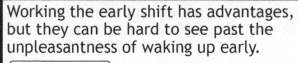

Working the early shift has advantages, but they can be hard to see past the unpleasantness of waking up early.

Why does your alarm play Miley Cyrus?

It gives me incentive to get up and turn it off quickly.

You could hit the snooze button.

And hear her again in five minutes? No thanks.

The first hour of an early morning can be rough, but there are tools available to help you cope.

That's, like, your third cup of coffee.

Fifth. Coffee allows me to perform my duties at peak efficiency.

That much coffee just makes me go to the bathroom.

That is one of my duties.

Once you're awake, you get things done without interruptions or distractions.

So, why'd you come in early?

To monkey with the projector. You?

To shuffle the boss's files.

Cool. I hate getting up early, but he's not going to sabotage himself.

Not as effectively as we can do it.

You'll also gain the respect of your supervisors and coworkers who come in to find you already hard at work.

I have to dig out files to research my big PowerPoint presentation tonight.

You should have come in early.

Yeah, tell me about it.

We'd rather not.

basicinstructions.net

People mistake being a gentleman with being polite. Sadly, you can be very polite without being a gentleman at all.

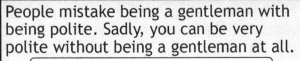

"Abby, you are cordially invited to my condo, where you will be generously subjected to my physical advances."

Cordial enough?

Oh, it's plenty cordial, but who's Abby?

First name on the list. I made one for every common female name.

Unlike mere manners, all gentlemanly behavior is designed to accomplish one purpose. To make women like you.

These make it seem like all you want from women is sex.

Which is true.

But you don't tell them that.

You're saying I should lie.

I'm saying to treat women like you respect them.

Which, in your case, is lying.

In order to act "like a gentleman," you need only treat a woman "like a lady."

Do you open doors for your dates?

Even if I have to crowd past them to do it.

Pull out their chairs?

Great chance to look at some butt.

Do you walk arm-in-arm with them?

You'd be surprised what I can feel with my elbow.

Women like a gentleman. Notice that I said "like," not "are attracted to."

My boyfriend blew me off last night.

Of course he did. He's an ass.

He was rude about it, too.

Of course he was. He's an ass.

I'm just so into him!

Of course you are. He's an ass.

basicinstructions.net

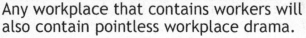

Any workplace that contains workers will also contain pointless workplace drama.

I am SO angry!

I'm sure you are.

OH, so you heard what's going on!

No, I just know you well enough to be sure that at any given moment you're probably angry.

Workplace drama is like a virus, in that it grows by drawing in new people. Try not to get "infected" yourself.

Jenkins has been going around bad-mouthing me behind my back.

It's a shame we can't discuss it.

This is the perfect time to discuss it.

Because ...

Jenkins isn't here.

Naturally.

You can avoid drama the same way you'd avoid a virus, by avoiding contact, effectively quarantining yourself.

I won't do this.

Do what?

Talk about Jenkins behind his back. It's exactly what he did to you.

He started it!

I'm just getting even.

That's better?

It feels better.

Of course, both viruses and workplace drama will sometimes mutate and infect those who thought they were immune.

I heard you were mean to Kate.

I told her I didn't want to talk about how you insulted her.

Yeah, I said she was "too sensitive."

I guess she is a bit oversensitive.

DOES IT MAKE YOU FEEL BIG TO PICK ON POOR KATE WHEN SHE'S NOT HERE TO DEFEND HERSELF?!

basicinstructions.net

BASIC INSTRUCTIONS

How to Handle a Surprising Truth

by Scott MEYER

Surprising truths can often spring from small observations that make you think about things you've never considered.

Remember Soundwave?

The transformer tape deck? Carried smaller transformers inside him? He was awesome!

I just realized, when he'd "eject" the smaller Transformers, it was like he was having babies.

Still awesome, just in a very different way.

Often these new ideas will lead you to realize things that are obvious, but that you, or anyone else, had never realized.

And if Soundwave had babies, that means SHE was a woman.

But there was nothing feminine about Soundwave! He was boxy and he sounded like a Speak & Spell.

Maybe that's what Transformer dudes like. It's a different culture, man. Don't judge.

Dealing with the ramifications of a new truth may make you uncomfortable.

I just can't accept that Transformers had different genders. It's too weird.

Less weird than the idea that Optimus Prime was a hermaphrodite?

Okay. Soundwave was a woman. So what?

Remember that discomfort. You'll see it mirrored in the people with whom you share your new-found knowledge.

You are, of course, insane.

Just because I believe a toy tape recorder that turned into a robot was actually a sexy lady, that means I'm crazy?!

You know what? Never mind.

If you're about to e-mail me to tell me there was a female Autobot in the Transformers animated movie, please don't. To do so would demean us both. basicinstructions.net

 Yeah. It turns out that there were many female Transformers. In fact, there's a Wikipedia page that is a list of female Transformers. There I learned that Moonracer was the romantic interest of Powerglide. You'd think I'd remember something like that.

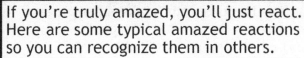

If you're truly amazed, you'll just react. Here are some typical amazed reactions so you can recognize them in others.

The Emperor has Rocket Hat chained up.

All the way up! I've never seen so many chains!

We don't discuss the Emperor's disturbingly vast collection of chains and restraints.

Why not?

We're afraid he'll chain us up.

Shocked Surprise: The most common reaction. Used when what the subject's seeing is the last thing they expected.

Three sets of handcuffs, two sets of leg irons, a 100-lb lead ball and a Hannibal Lecter mask, all on one man!

And he STILL managed to get the Emperor in a headlock.

Stunned Admiration: Subject is impressed to the highest degree. Marked by talking in low tones and inability to look away.

It wouldn't have occurred to me to use the hat rocket's exhaust as a blowtorch.

I would've wasted time using the torch on the chains, instead of the Emperor's head.

OW! FINE! I'll unlock you! GEEZ!

Outrage: The opposite of stunned admiration. A heady mixture of equal parts shock and anger.

Why didn't you help me?!

You get into these situations so often, I figured you were, you know, "into it."

Ooooh, I can't wait to get you all chained up!

You see my point.

SILENCE!!

© 2010: Scott Meyer

basicinstructions.net

9

BASIC INSTRUCTIONS

How to Solve an Intractable Social Issue

by Scott MEYER

Important things are seldom done alone. Assemble a team of dedicated, like-minded people to tackle the problem.

I have an idea that could make the world a better place.

Is your idea to never have another of your stupid ideas?

You didn't have to insult me.

Actually, I was trying to use logic to make your head explode.

Define the problem. Make sure you and your team know what the problem is, and what would constitute a solution.

Everyone agrees, teenage promiscuity is a problem.

Everyone except every teenage boy I've ever met.

Everyone agrees, teenage pregnancy is a problem.

Continue.

To truly solve the problem, you have to discover and attack its root cause.

The most likely cause is that toys glamorize parenthood, making it look like fun.

Or, teenagers are prone to powerful biological urges and suffer a profound lack of foresight.

Whatever. Here's my toy idea.

Once the cause is known, try to design a solution that is simple, effective and if at all possible, outrageously profitable.

It's a toy baby stroller. Pushing it powers a siren that sounds like a baby yelling.

Will parents buy something that's irritating just because it's educational?

Did you own a See 'n Say?

Does the cow go moo?

basicinstructions.net

BASIC INSTRUCTIONS

How to Deal with a Bad Day

by Scott MEYER

Everybody has bad days. Trying to deny a day's essential badness will only cause it to escalate until you cannot ignore it.

How was the meeting?

The client insulted me for a full hour.

Oh. I'll be sure to attend the next meeting with him.

So he'll be more respectful?

So we can tag-team insult you.

Get it off your chest. Talking about your problems often makes you feel better.

Can you believe he said that?

Yes, easily. He insults us with every paycheck.

True. Both with the amount he pays, and when he writes "parasite" in the memo field.

Find someone else who's having a bad day. You'll feel less alone, and maybe even a bit grateful that you aren't them.

I got a call from my daughter. She was driving distracted and totaled my car.

Texting?

No, she was taking her birth control pill.

You ARE having a bad day.

Now the counter-intuitive part. Try to cheer them up. Making them feel better invariably makes you feel better as well.

At least she wasn't hurt, and the pill does have benefits beyond birth control.

Like what?

It'll clear up her complexion, which'll make her more attractive to boys!

Thank God for that.

basicinstructions.net

BASIC INSTRUCTIONS

How to Refer to Someone's Not-Spouse

by Scott MEYER

Many couples are choosing not to marry. This is perfectly within their rights, but can be conversationally awkward.

How's your ... what do you call the woman you live with?

Vanessa.

That's her name, but is there something else you call her?

Honey-butt.

I'm not going to call her that.

Damn right you're not.

There are many words that can be used to refer to a non-married, romantically-linked cohabitator, but none quite fit.

Wife?

We're not married.

Common-law wife?

Too trailer park.

Partner?

Makes us sound like Crockett and Tubbs.

Boss?

I tried that, but she ordered me to stop.

Of course, you can simply ask a member of the couple what title they prefer.

Just call her my girlfriend.

I'm not comfortable with that.

I'd like to call her something that implies more commitment on your part.

I'm not comfortable with THAT.

Following the couple's lead will result in the least discomfort for everyone, but there will still be some discomfort.

If calling her my girlfriend is uncomfortable, you're welcome to refer to her as my soulmate.

Girlfriend it is.

basicinstructions.net

There has been confusion amongst my readers as to Jenkins' status. For the record, he's a divorced father. His ex-wife has custody and he is in a long-term, monogamous relationship but he's always on the hunt. He has not chosen monogamy. He has had it thrust upon him.

BASIC INSTRUCTIONS

How to Utilize Research to Maximize Chances for Success

by Scott MEYER

First, carefully select the field in which you intend to achieve your success.

First, I searched for a field of endeavor where anyone, regardless of their lack of skill, talent or taste has a chance of finding success.

I chose webcomics.

Of course.

Then, research that field, gathering as much information as possible. Analyze the data and draw useful conclusions.

Then, I studied what modern Americans find amusing. Sexual humor, geek and pop culture references, bathroom humor, and things talking that are not supposed to talk.

So you've cracked the MacFarlane code. Good for you.

Now devise a plan that uses the data as leverage to give you an advantage.

Here's my idea! What do you think?

NERVOUS BLADDER and IRRITABLE BOWEL

SAN DIEGO COMIC CON INTERNATIONAL

starring in

Comic-Con-Fusion

I think you're gonna be rich, and that I hate you.

Spend time honing your plan, making sure all bases are covered. Then execute the plan to the best of your abilities.

Where's the sex?

Booth-babes make Bladder nervous ... er.

Which makes Bowel more irritable, I suppose.

Yup! It writes itself!

I can see why you wouldn't want to take credit yourself.

basicinstructions.net

BASIC INSTRUCTIONS

How to Defend Your Skills

by Scott MEYER

No matter how self-evident your skills are, eventually they will be questioned.

I'll drive.

Nah, I can.

Nonsense. It's my turn!

Don't worry about it.

I insist.

Fine, you drive. I'll follow you in my car.

The best way to defend your skills is to demonstrate them. If this is not possible, try a logic-based verbal defense.

I am an excellent driver. I've driven way more miles than you. I've never received a moving violation, and all five of my vehicles that've been totaled were in non-at-fault accidents.

So I should let you drive because you're experienced and unlucky.

Of course, you should listen to criticism. It is possible that there's a hole in your skill set of which you weren't aware.

Your driving makes me sick.

Sick from jealousy.

No, from seasickness. It's the lurchy way you hit the gas pedal.

I've determined that's the most efficient way to drive.

If the goal is to create vomit, then yes.

If you find their criticisms to be without merit, don't hesitate to say so. Humoring petty sniping helps nobody.

So the problem's not that I'm a bad driver, it's that you aren't a skilled enough passenger to withstand my advanced driving techniques.

You're welcome to think whatever you want.

As long as you think it from the passenger seat.

basicinstructions.net

I have a perfect driving record. No moving violations. No at-fault accidents. Still, people don't enjoy riding in a car I am driving. Somehow, I don't instill confidence. When I was learning, my mom took me out to practice once. When I asked again, she answered that she'd "had enough."

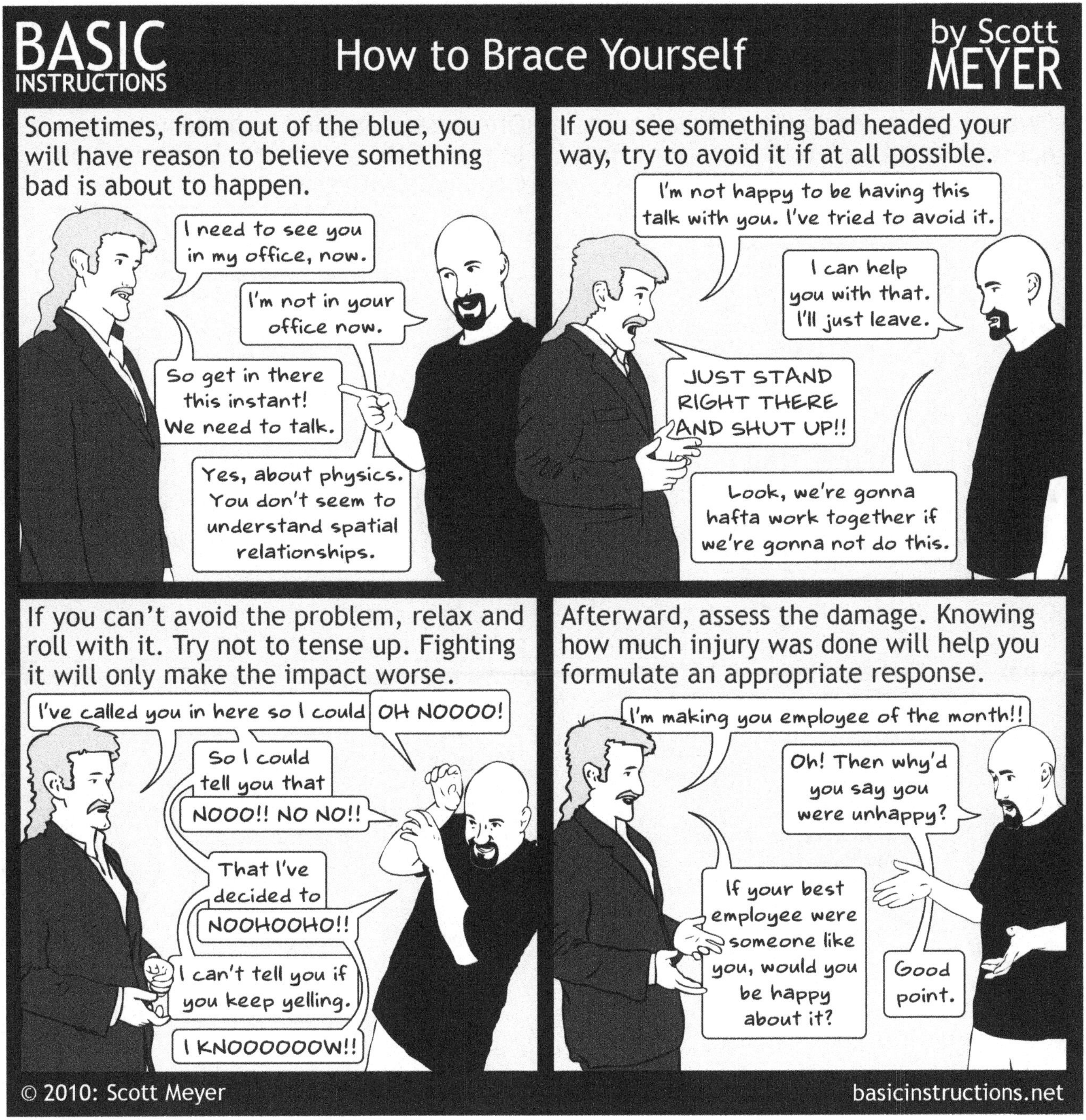
BASIC INSTRUCTIONS
How to Brace Yourself
by Scott MEYER
Sometimes, from out of the blue, you will have reason to believe something bad is about to happen.
I need to see you in my office, now.
I'm not in your office now.
So get in there this instant! We need to talk.
Yes, about physics. You don't seem to understand spatial relationships.
If you see something bad headed your way, try to avoid it if at all possible.
I'm not happy to be having this talk with you. I've tried to avoid it.
I can help you with that. I'll just leave.
JUST STAND RIGHT THERE AND SHUT UP!!
Look, we're gonna hafta work together if we're gonna not do this.
If you can't avoid the problem, relax and roll with it. Try not to tense up. Fighting it will only make the impact worse.
I've called you in here so I could
OH NOOOO!
So I could tell you that
NOOO!! NO NO!!
That I've decided to
NOOHOOHO!!
I can't tell you if you keep yelling.
I KNOOOOOOW!!
Afterward, assess the damage. Knowing how much injury was done will help you formulate an appropriate response.
I'm making you employee of the month!!
Oh! Then why'd you say you were unhappy?
If your best employee were someone like you, would you be happy about it?
Good point.
© 2010: Scott Meyer
basicinstructions.net

"What's bothering you" can be a hard question to answer, because often when it's asked, nothing is bothering you.

What's bothering you?

Nothing.

You look unhappy.

I'm happy. This is my happy face.

That must be terribly depressing.

Of course, your first impulse will be to tell them that nothing is bothering you. Good luck with that.

Seriously, what's wrong?

Nothing! I'm smiling!

Yeah, but it's one of those "if you keep talking to me I may lose it" kinda smiles.

You see those a lot, don't you?

Of course, if something is actually bothering you, you can just tell them what it is. Perhaps they can help.

It's someone here at work.

Yeah?

I was in a fine mood, then he comes up ...

Yeah?

And asks me what's wrong.

What happened then?

I insulted him, and he didn't get it.

HA! What an idiot.

Or, you can just make something up to get them to leave you alone.

You're right. Something's bothering me. I've never told you this, but I was born with a deformity.

My face is on the side of my head. As long as you've known me, I've been looking to the left.

I didn't know.

Nobody here does, but feel free to spread the word.

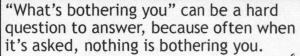 There's that old saying, "If you don't know who the dumbest person in the room is, it's probably you." The same thing goes for figuring out what's bothering me at any given moment.

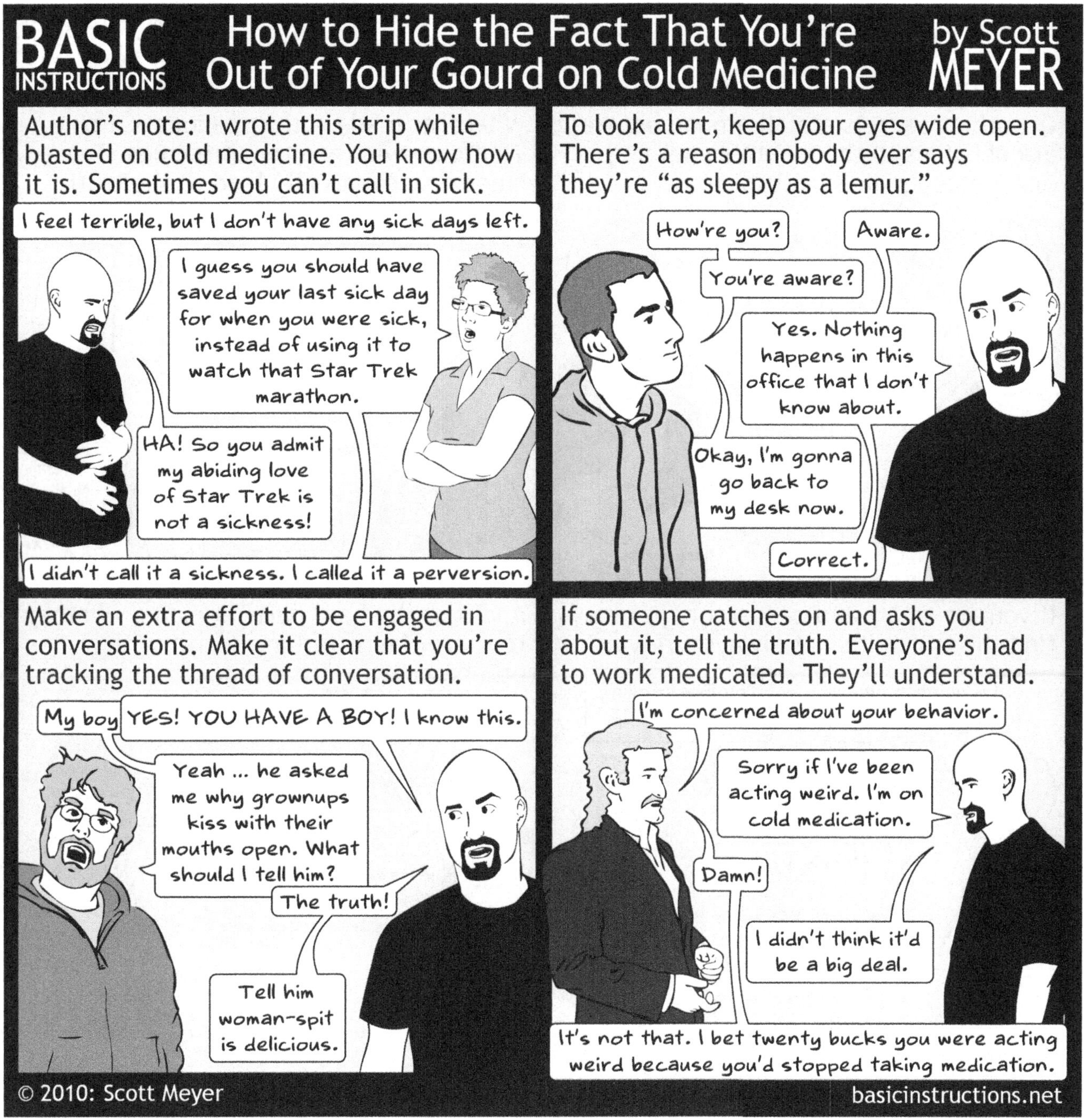
BASIC INSTRUCTIONS
How to Hide the Fact That You're Out of Your Gourd on Cold Medicine
by Scott MEYER
Author's note: I wrote this strip while blasted on cold medicine. You know how it is. Sometimes you can't call in sick.
I feel terrible, but I don't have any sick days left.
I guess you should have saved your last sick day for when you were sick, instead of using it to watch that Star Trek marathon.
HA! So you admit my abiding love of Star Trek is not a sickness!
I didn't call it a sickness. I called it a perversion.
To look alert, keep your eyes wide open. There's a reason nobody ever says they're "as sleepy as a lemur."
How're you?
Aware.
You're aware?
Yes. Nothing happens in this office that I don't know about.
Okay, I'm gonna go back to my desk now.
Correct.
Make an extra effort to be engaged in conversations. Make it clear that you're tracking the thread of conversation.
My boy
YES! YOU HAVE A BOY! I know this.
Yeah ... he asked me why grownups kiss with their mouths open. What should I tell him?
The truth!
Tell him woman-spit is delicious.
If someone catches on and asks you about it, tell the truth. Everyone's had to work medicated. They'll understand.
I'm concerned about your behavior.
Sorry if I've been acting weird. I'm on cold medication.
Damn!
I didn't think it'd be a big deal.
It's not that. I bet twenty bucks you were acting weird because you'd stopped taking medication.
© 2010: Scott Meyer
basicinstructions.net

Disturbing secrets are all around us. We are oblivious to them until something unexpected makes us suspicious.

You look happy.

Yes, I do! Is that a problem?

Usually.

Whatever made you suspicious is a clue. That clue will lead to more clues. Those clues may eventually lead to the truth.

Wanna know why I'm happy?

I'm not sure.

I want to tell you.

Then I probably don't.

Want a hint?

Maybe.

Smell me.

I don't want a hint, or anything else, that badly.

If you are smart and persistent, you may find the truth. It's not always a reward.

I'm using a new peppermint soap.

You like smelling minty. I get it.

I don't just smell minty. I feel minty.

Yeah, I get it.

The more sensitive my parts are, the mintier they feel.

EWWWWWWW!

Now you get it.

And now the hard part. Deciding whether to share the disturbing secret with others, or live with it alone.

He said more, but I don't want to burden you.

I don't see what he could have said that was so bad.

He said it was as if his erogenous zones had eaten an Altoid.

That wasn't an invitation to tell me.

basicinstructions.net

There are people who don't get this particular comic. If you are one of them, try showering with a bar of Dr. Bronner's peppermint soap. I'm not promising that afterward you'll find the comic funny, just that you'll understand it better.

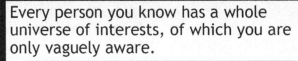

BASIC INSTRUCTIONS

How to Learn About Other People's Interests

by Scott MEYER

Every person you know has a whole universe of interests, of which you are only vaguely aware.

I have to swing by the dry cleaner tonight and pick up my costume for this weekend.

If you don't tell me what you're doing, I'm just gonna assume that you're a furvert.

I'm happy to tell you.

Good. I'll still probably assume you're a furvert.

They may tell you about their outside interests. It likely won't seem interesting to you, but it's still worth listening.

I'm a Civil War reenactor.

Ah, the heady combination of camping, violence, and playing pretend.

I also wear fake muttonchop sideburns.

Are you sure you wouldn't rather be a furvert?

You may be surprised to find that their seemingly uninteresting hobby is more compelling than you'd thought possible.

Recreating battles from the past gives us a better appreciation for the incredible hardships our forefathers had to endure.

I can see how that'd be inspiring.

It really is! I hope we don't get rained out this time.

Or, you might find that their interests are not so out of the ordinary after all.

That's not so weird! I'm a Korean War reenactor.

For the last time, putting on a Hawaiian shirt, drinking martinis, and mooning over your autographed photo of Loretta Swit does not make you a Korean War reenactor.

I also wear a fake moustache.

basicinstructions.net

Panel 1

We all have hidden fears that can affect our behavior in surprising ways.

Hey, let's go to Gatorland!

Good God, WHY?!

'Cause they've got alligators.

That's not a reason to go somewhere! That's reason to avoid going somewhere!

You'd like to go to "Gatorless-Land."

That, or just stay home.

Panel 2

The obvious fears everyone shares are seldom the problem. It's the small ones that are yours alone that get you.

I promise, all the animals are kept in cages.

Okay, I'll go.

There's a huge cage full of hundreds of tiny songbirds, where you walk in and they land on you.

I didn't finish. Okay, I'll go watch TV while you perish in a fluttering mass of winged terror.

Panel 3

Many fears are irrational. Often a logical analysis of the fear will nullify it. Often, but not always.

But tiny birds are harmless.

A tiny bird is harmless. You said there're hundreds! Hundreds of anything can be dangerous.

That's the least convincing thing you've ever said.

We'll see if you still feel that way after I've said it hundreds of times.

Panel 4

The only way to gain lasting mastery of your fear is to face it, and demonstrate that it's not actually that bad.

Aw, they love you!

THEY SENSE MY FEAR!

That one is licking you!

IT'S TASTING MY FEAR!

Well I'm having fun.

YOU'RE ENJOYING MY FEAR!

True.

After I published this comic, I was criticized for promoting Gatorland. Reading it again years later, I'm still not sure that I did.

We all try to be good friends, but sometimes our approach is misguided.

At least you've finally hit rock bottom. Your life can't possibly get worse.

I don't think that's true. Things could certainly get worse!

Now, now. Pessimism never helps anything.

An outside observer can look at your behavior with fresh eyes and point out ways you could be a better friend.

You shouldn't kick Rick when he's down.

The guy's always down! When else am I gonna kick him?

How about when I'm out of hearing range?

It's best to try to be the sort of friend you'd want: supportive but honest.

My point is, you can still spring back to life, like a possum.

You could've said "like a phoenix."

A phoenix is a majestic bird made of fire. A possum is a helpless, frightened animal. Which do you think describes you better?

Your friend knows what they need better than you possibly could. Pay attention to them, and they'll tell you what to do.

OR BRINE SHRIMP! They look like dirt, then you put 'em in water and they turn into disgusting lice-like creatures!

Please stop encouraging me.

SEE! Missy just doesn't understand how man-friendship works!

And you don't understand how human hearing works.

Ah, brine shrimp, also known as "Sea Monkeys." They're one of the great educational toys of all time, especially if you're trying to teach your children about misleading advertising.

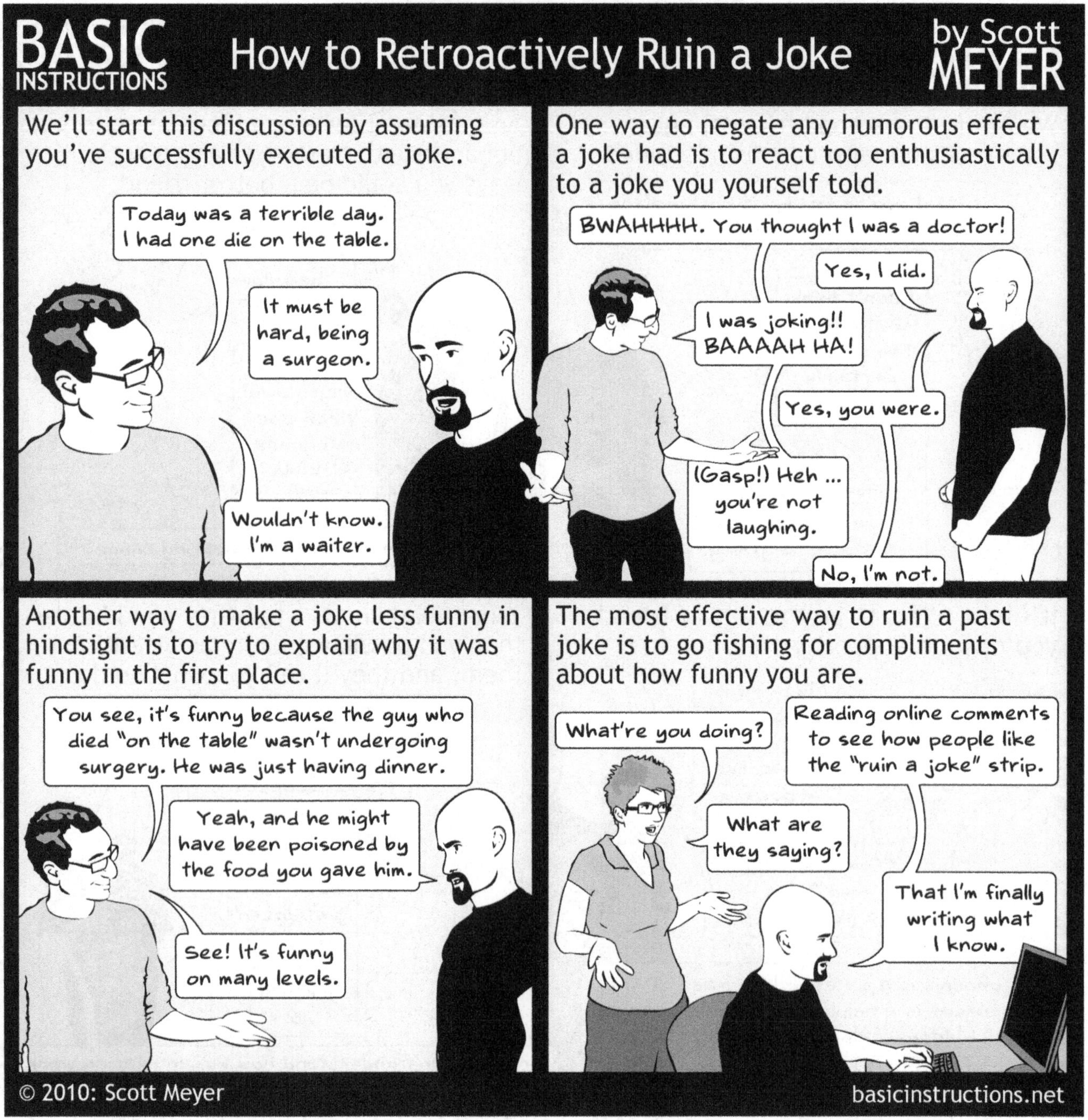
BASIC INSTRUCTIONS
How to Retroactively Ruin a Joke
by Scott MEYER
We'll start this discussion by assuming you've successfully executed a joke.
Today was a terrible day. I had one die on the table.
It must be hard, being a surgeon.
Wouldn't know. I'm a waiter.
One way to negate any humorous effect a joke had is to react too enthusiastically to a joke you yourself told.
BWAHHHH. You thought I was a doctor!
Yes, I did.
I was joking!! BAAAAH HA!
Yes, you were.
(Gasp!) Heh ... you're not laughing.
No, I'm not.
Another way to make a joke less funny in hindsight is to try to explain why it was funny in the first place.
You see, it's funny because the guy who died "on the table" wasn't undergoing surgery. He was just having dinner.
Yeah, and he might have been poisoned by the food you gave him.
See! It's funny on many levels.
The most effective way to ruin a past joke is to go fishing for compliments about how funny you are.
What're you doing?
Reading online comments to see how people like the "ruin a joke" strip.
What are they saying?
That I'm finally writing what I know.
© 2010: Scott Meyer
basicinstructions.net

People may have an image of themselves they wish to project. One way to sell this image is a carefully selected nickname.

Here comes The Maverick!

Who the $*$# is "The Maverick?"

I'm The Maverick, 'cause I do things other people won't.

Yes. For example, nobody else will ever call you "the Maverick."

Be sure to choose a nickname that is evocative of the values, attitude and behavior for which you are known.

The Maverick plays by his own rules.

True! I've seen your rules in action.

Rule one: Do what you're told.

Rule two: Whine about it endlessly.

Rule three: If your boss is in the room, disregard rule two.

Of course, for the nickname to do any good, you must get others to use it.

Nobody calls you The Maverick.

Yet!

I'll make you a deal. I'll call you The Maverick if you call me whatever I want.

The Maverick has no problem with that.

Yet!

Your name can change how people view you, but over time your actions will change how people view your name.

Later:

So, how's The Maverick today?

Fine, Scott.

That's not what you call me.

It's not worth being called The Maverick if I have to call you "Sir."

Just say it sarcastically, like it's an insult. That's what I do ... The Maverick.

basicinstructions.net

I did, in fact, meet a guy who insisted upon being called "The Maverick." I assumed he wanted to be associated with John McCain or the movie Top Gun, but when I heard the name Maverick, I pictured the Chevy my grandmother drove.

Most of us love food, but describing food in an appetizing way can be challenging.

Man! I've seen some offended waiters before, but that was amazing.

I was trying to be complimentary.

That's why it was so amazing.

Start by describing the food as an object. Say what it is and what it is made of.

What did you order again?

I ordered the beefmeat balls.

Yeah, that was a typo. You aren't meant to actually call them that.

THEY'RE BALLS! MADE OF MEAT! BEEF ... MEAT!

If you wish to be more descriptive, you can mention how the food was prepared.

When you saw you'd offended him and started backpedaling, that was awesome.

I just said I was sure they were well made.

You said "I'm certain the beefmeat has been exquisitely balled."

Other subjects you can touch on are the quality of the ingredients, and the care taken in the dish's preparation.

The best part was when you said "You can tell the chef hand-balls the finest beefmeat available."

No. In retrospect the best part was when you said "I'll tip you fifty bucks if you don't tell the chef about this conversation."

basicinstructions.net

BASIC INSTRUCTIONS

How to Interrogate a Suspect

by Scott MEYER

All suspects need to be interrogated, but some call for an interrogator who has special techniques and expertise.

We found the guy who planned the big bank job. Would you interrogate him, Omnipresent Man?

Wise of you to utilize my skills in this case.

Eh, really it's that you're already in the interrogation room. Just seems convenient.

When interrogating a suspect, start from a dominant position of strength.

I know you planned the bank job.

Of course you do, Omnipresent Man. You were there for the whole thing.

Right! So there's no point in not telling me.

But I don't see much point in telling you either.

If sheer dominance doesn't work, a more subtle approach is to use logic to trap them into giving you what you want.

TALK!

Okay! You knew all about the heist and didn't stop it.

You're an accessory!

SHUT UP!

If you've exhausted your arsenal of tricks without success, it's time to confer with your colleagues.

He has a good point, Omnipresent Man. Give me one good reason not to arrest you.

Why bother? Are you gonna send me to jail?

I'M ALREADY THERE!!

basicinstructions.net

They say that it's very difficult to make a compelling story about Superman because his powers make it almost impossible to ever defeat him. Writing for Omnipresent Man poses a similar problem, which I have solved by making him a lazy coward. Effectively, he is his own Kryptonite.

When a new person is introduced to an office, someone must show them around. Often that someone is you.

You're not doing anything important. Why don't you show Athena how things work around here?

Hello.

Welcome. You've just learned your first two lessons.

"Always look busy," and "you're not important."

Though you'll want to remain positive, it is imperative that you warn them of dangers and pitfalls they should avoid.

Jenkins there has no knowledge that can help you. Even if he has knowledge, it can't help you.

So he plays dumb.

Please, he's a professional. He works dumb.

Many things are difficult to fully describe verbally, and must be demonstrated.

Graham here is a single, heterosexual male, and you are cute, so everything he does'll be a transparent attempt to impress you.

Please, I treat all my many lady-friends with equal respect and ... uh ... classy-ness.

Yeah, I see what you mean.

The better you prepare your new co-worker, the sooner they will be up to speed, which benefits you *and* them.

I'm trapped in a toxic environment, surrounded by incompetents who are also trapped.

This must be how Boba Fett felt when he fell into the Sarlacc pit.

You're gonna fit in just fine.

YOU TAKE THAT BACK!!

basicinstructions.net

BASIC INSTRUCTIONS

How to Cover for Your Own Ignorance

by Scott MEYER

Panel 1

Everyone has subjects in which they are ignorant. It's hard to admit this to others, and harder to admit to ourselves.

This meeting's gonna suck, but I can't get out of it.

You're like the battleship Bismarck.

Is that a fat joke?

NO! It's a historical reference.

DAMN! At least I'd understand a fat joke.

Panel 2

One way to hide your ignorance is to immediately change the subject to something you know better.

The sinking of the Bismarck was similar to the battle at Mutara Nebula from Star Trek two.

You can't compare a real battle to Star Trek!

You can't, because you're falling prey to two-dimensional thinking.

Panel 3

Or you can use trickery to con someone else into telling you about the subject.

What would you say was the most interesting thing about the Bismarck?

That you don't want to admit that you know nothing about it.

I don't find that interesting.

Everyone else in the office will.

Panel 4

Today's most popular method: self-righteousness. Act offended and chastise them for knowing things they shouldn't.

Don't try to guilt me for not knowing history,

I'M AN AMERICAN!

My forefathers fought and died so I'd have the right to have no idea where or when they fought and died!

basicinstructions.net

 I think the Bismarck had a torpedo damage its rudders, leaving it aimed at enemy ships and unable to steer away. I know for a fact that in the Mutara Nebula, Spock realized Khan had forgotten the third axis, allowing the Enterprise to rise behind him and take the upper hand.

BASIC INSTRUCTIONS — How to Appreciate American Cuisine
by Scott MEYER

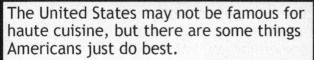

Panel 1:

The United States may not be famous for haute cuisine, but there are some things Americans just do best.

When I was in Paris, the food was AMAZING!

Yeah, French chefs are good for certain things, but I've yet to see one who could make a decent Oreo.

Panel 2:

Instead of focusing on areas where America may lag behind, revel in the American areas of expertise.

We just make some things better. Like a Big Mac.

Any chef can make a good burger.

A Big Mac isn't a good burger, but it is a great Big Mac.

That's a dubious argument.

Another thing we Americans make well.

Panel 3:

Note: some regions, specific restaurants, and even particular chefs may be the best in the world at individual dishes.

So they made a mediocre burger and called it something new. Good for them.

They also have great fries and the world's best Diet Coke.

How can they have the best Diet Coke?!

That's their secret. I think the large-bore drinking straw has something to do with it.

Panel 4:

As with all countries, America's approach to food is reflective of its approach to life, and should be celebrated.

"If you can't do something right, call it something different."

That's a pretty crappy philosophy.

True, but it's a great mission statement.

basicinstructions.net

One of life's most surprisingly difficult tasks is to make a simple decision with another human being.

Wanna get lunch?

YES! LUNCH!

Third most important meal of the day! It ends the fiasco that was your morning and sets the tone for the fiasco that is your afternoon!

Where do you wanna go?

Don't care.

The best first move is to decide what you think should be done and propose that.

Quiznos?

Nah, they heat their sandwiches.

Blimpie?

Nah, they don't heat their sandwiches.

Subway?

Nah, they heat some of their sandwiches.

So, you don't want a sandwich.

I didn't say that.

That's the problem.

If that doesn't work, find out what the other party wants to do and try to find a mutually acceptable way to do it.

What sounds good?

Everything.

King's Spork Buffet has everything. Huge, steamy piles of it, heat-lamped to perfection, heaped under a sneeze guard.

Good work. Everything no longer sounds good.

If all else fails, force the other party to make a decision, then adapt to it.

You pick a place.

Whatever you want.

All right then! 7-Eleven it is.

I refuse to eat at 7-Eleven.

Then that's definitely where I'm going.

basicinstructions.net

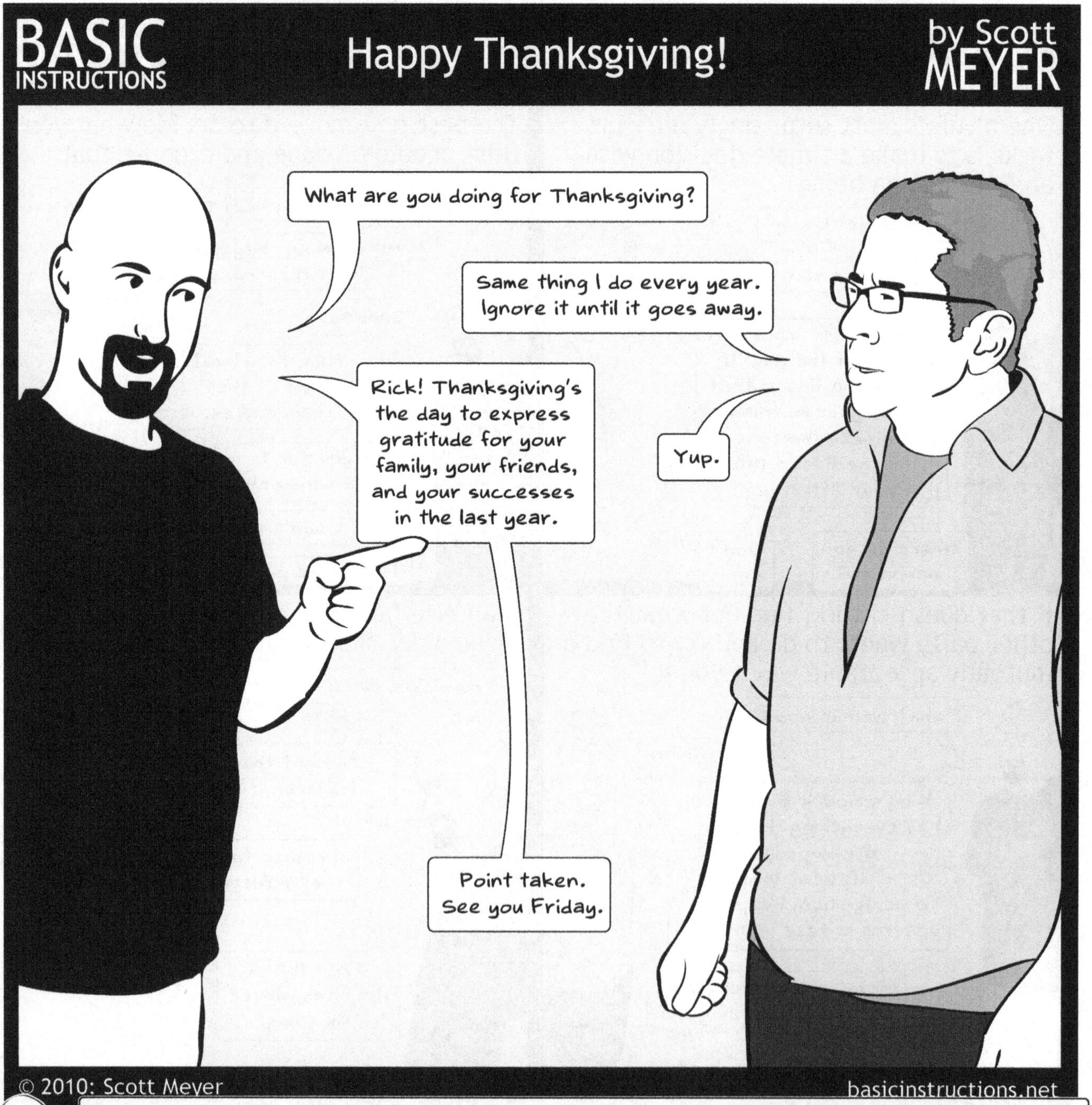
BASIC INSTRUCTIONS
Happy Thanksgiving!
by Scott MEYER
What are you doing for Thanksgiving?
Same thing I do every year. Ignore it until it goes away.
Rick! Thanksgiving's the day to express gratitude for your family, your friends, and your successes in the last year.
Yup.
Point taken. See you Friday.
© 2010: Scott Meyer
basicinstructions.net

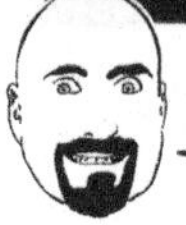

I just want to take a moment to yet again point out that I've offered to lay off of Rick in the comic, but every time I suggest it, the real Rick refuses to hear of it and insists that I keep going. It seems he enjoys the punishment, disturbing as that idea may be.

How to Criticize Someone You Respect Deeply

Nobody is above criticism, even those you admire. Start by establishing that you respect this person, and why.

George Lucas is a great man. He ignited the imaginations of a generation, changed the way movies are made, and pioneered the use of a beard to create the illusion of a strong jaw.

Truly, he has accomplished much.

Every great person has obvious failings. Mention them quickly and move on to more interesting topics.

But it must be said: he writes stilted dialog, created Jar Jar, and is responsible for a generation of men trying to use beards to create the illusion of a strong jaw.

Truly, he has much to answer for.

Focus on less obvious failings that add something new to the discourse and show that you've given the topic due thought.

Only the Jedi use the Force, and they only use it for good. If Anakin was supposed to "bring balance to the Force," logically he'd have to be tremendously evil.

Yoda should have killed him on sight.

Then they wouldn't have had two more movies.

I didn't say Yoda should've killed him quickly.

To be worthy of respect, a public figure must withstand criticism gracefully.

You guys are right. George Lucas sucks.

TAKE THAT BACK!

But you just said

SILENCE!

HOW DARE YOU INSULT GEORGE LUCAS!

YOU, WHO WEAR HIS BEARD!!

basicinstructions.net

If a coworker is acting strangely, talk to them to determine if they're impaired.

Judging by your behavior and aroma, you're either suffering a cold, or drunk on a cocktail that includes menthol and eucalyptus.

Why can't it be both?

Once you know they're impaired, make sure that they know they're impaired.

You're acting kinda dopey.

IMPOSSIBLE!

I'll have you know the bottle said "Non-drowsy."

Are you drowsy?

NOPE!

Next time you should get "non-dopey" formula.

If their judgment has been affected, it may take some work to convince them.

I am not dopey! I'm ... what word means the opposite of dopey?

I'd argue that if you don't know what word means the opposite of dopey, you really shouldn't use that word to describe yourself.

Once all that is established, keep an eye on your coworker and prevent them from making any embarrassing mistakes.

Do you want to go to dinner tonight?

Yes, I do.

He means with him.

LORD NO!

OH! I get it now! Men go out with women who act dopey because they can!

That's right! Your medicine must be wearing off.

© 2010: Scott Meyer

basicinstructions.net

From time to time we all have a need to persuade somebody of something.

It's time for the client's yearly "please don't fire us" briefing.

But he comes in every month.

Those are the monthly "please don't fire us" briefings.

What's the difference?

Expect him to be twelve times angrier.

Books, magazines, and the internet are all full of tricks and gimmicks you can use to try to influence people's thinking.

I've got the intimidating tall chair and the PowerPoint slides with the confusing bullet points. Also, I intend to make constant, intrusive eye contact.

What about the hypno-wheel?

I built that into the PowerPoint.

Way to streamline the efficiencies!

OOH! That'd make a good bullet point!

At the end of the day, nothing works better than a clear, simple message that makes logical sense, delivered calmly.

We've earned your business by streamlining efficiencies, maximizing our negative potential...

EFFICIENCIES? STREAMLINED!

NEG POTENTIAL? MAXIMIZED!

...and making you sleeeeeepy. Veeeeeery sleeeeeepy!

Sadly, some people simply will not be persuaded, no matter what you do.

I wish you idiots put this much effort into actually doing the work I pay you to do.

We do, with roughly the same results.

They say that LBJ had a special chair installed in Air Force One that was higher than all the other seats. The press called it "The King Chair." The Secret Service called it "The Throne." I like that the Secret Service used the correct word and the professional writers did not.

BASIC INSTRUCTIONS

How to "Get Your Head Around" an Unbelievable Fact

by Scott MEYER

The world is full of facts, and our brains are limited. Sometimes we learn things that our brains can't quite process.

I learned something today that I just can't get my head around.

I was talking to a guy. He said he's from Puerto Rico.

Yes, there's an island called Puerto Rico that's not a state, but NOT THAT!!!

If something is clearly true despite your preconceived notions, accept it. It's true whether you believe it or not.

At first I thought I'd misheard him. He said he drinks "coffee and cheese."

So he drinks coffee and eats cheese. So what?

NO! He puts cheddar cheese in his coffee.

I'm sorry. I must've misheard you.

Focus not on the troublesome fact, but on yourself. Try to figure out why you're having so much trouble accepting it.

Apparently it's a common thing in Puerto Rico.

I love coffee. I love cheese, but the idea of combining them horrifies me.

It's like if someone made a cocktail of whisky and ranch dressing.

When are you gonna let that go? I was in college.

Working to understand new information improves your mind, and makes it easier to process difficult facts in the future.

I know a guy from Brazil who puts mayonnaise on pizza.

Has he ever been punished for this?

Well, he eats the pizza, if that's what you mean.

basicinstructions.net

Yes, I know a Puerto Rican who puts cheese in her coffee. I also know a Brazilian who puts mayonnaise on his pizza. My mom used to roll Spam in crumbled saltine crackers and fry it, then I would eat it. Who am I to judge?

First, publicly declare your intention to get revenge. It's good sportsmanship, and it terrorizes your adversary.

I will have my revenge!

REVEEEEEENGE!

Will your revenge be damaging my ears by yelling "revenge"?

PERHAAAPS!

Then, bide your time. Fade into the background until the adversary forgets about you and lowers their guard.

Is that it?

For now. Revenge is a dish best served cold.

They also say living well is the best revenge.

Indeed. Some day when you least expect it, I will live well.

It's easy to become distracted. The trick is to allow the adversary's attention to lapse while you stay focused on revenge.

Know what else is best served cold? Gazpacho.

That's true. Gazpacho is the revenge of soup. They should call it that.

Nobody'd order a bowl of "revenge soup."

Your patience will be rewarded. Some day they will be vulnerable, and it will be time to wreak your revenge.

Remember last year, you suggested they should call gazpacho "revenge soup," and I made you feel like an idiot?

Sounds familiar. What a dumb idea! "Revenge soup." I can't believe I said something that idiotic!

VENGEANCE IS MINE!

© 2010: Scott Meyer

basicinstructions.net

35

Creating hypothetical businesses is fun, and excellent mental exercise. Start with a simple idea that is inarguably true.

What's the scariest theme for a roller coaster?

A runaway Wrong! The answer is: "poorly maintained roller coaster."

Sparks and visible rust can make the safest ride terrifying.

You got this idea from your car, didn't you?

Expand on the idea until you think of a business that capitalizes on it.

I'd make a whole park themed as an abandoned theme park.

Think of the money you'd save on cleaning!

It would help offset the tremendous cost of the liability lawyers.

Plan every aspect of the business, finding and solving problems as they arise.

The ride operators could be dressed as squatters and gang members!

Even the kiddie rides?

If a kid lives with the kinda parents who'd take them to "Abandoned Land," a fake squatter in a clown nose isn't gonna faze them.

Whether the idea you develop is useful or not, the process of thinking it through will be rewarding.

Then, every night there'd be a stunt and fireworks show where the gangs and the squatters fight for control of the park!

This is by far the best idea you've ever had.

You think it would work?

Oh, Lord no!

basicinstructions.net

PSAs work best when the audience feels that they know and trust the presenter. If you can afford it, get a celebrity.

Hello. I'm Scott Meyer, the creator of Basic Instructions.

I'm speaking to you today because I couldn't afford to get a celebrity.

Once you have the audience's attention, explain the problem about which you're trying to raise awareness.

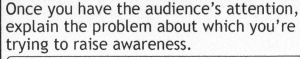

Alarmingly soon it will be 2012, and the copyright date in the corner of the comic will be changing.

I make comics up to a month before they're posted, so there'll be a delay before you see the new copyright date. Take a moment. Breathe ...

Yawn, if you like.

Once the problem is established, lay out the problem's consequences in a clear, emotionally impactful manner.

I know this issue is important because every year I receive countless corrections if the new date doesn't show up immediately!!

It seems the copyright date is one of the comic's prime attractions!! People gather to bask in the glory of a four-digit number and a little C in a circle!

Calm down.

YES! EVERYONE CALM DOWN!!

Now tell them what they can do to help. People are good. If they see a problem and know how to fix it, they usually will.

This January, when the copyright date still says "2011," please remember that there's a delay. If you still need to complain, feel free to tell your case worker, AA sponsor, or legal guardian.

ANYBODY BUT ME!

There's no need for insults!

SHE'S RIGHT! DON'T INSULT ME EITHER!!

basicinstructions.net

You may think I'm kidding, but I would receive e-mails every year. I'm fortunate to have highly intelligent, detail oriented readers who genuinely want to help me. It really is a great asset. I'm not claiming that I enjoy being corrected, mind you, just that I need it. Often.

For a story to generate suspense, it must be novel but believable. Make the situation possible, but highly unlikely.

I'm too sexy for my shirt. Too sexy for my shirt, so sexy it huuuuurts.

My phone is ringing. Someone wants to talk to me.

Using familiar situations is a shortcut when writing stories, but put a new spin on them to make the story original.

Rrrrrick-phone!

OH NOOOO ... wait, what call?

RICK! The call is coming from inside your house!

This call, the one we're having now.

Oh, okay then.

Ahem ... (cough) OOOOOOOOOOO!

Solve problems quickly, but make the solution create more and even worse problems. This draws the reader in.

Luckily, I'm not home.

What are you gonna do?

Wanna do the dishes?

I know, because I am at home. YOUR home, calling you from inside it!

Whatever I want.

No.

When you come to the end of the story, try to surprise the reader with a shock or twist they didn't anticipate.

Find anything embarrassing?

Dude, I had to hunt to find something that wasn't!

What about my set of first edition Harry Potter books? Those are cool.

They were before you went through them crossing out the name "Harry Potter" and writing in "Rick."

basicinstructions.net

Life is full of frustrations, and sometimes everyone just feels the need to vent.

What's bothering you?

You don't want to hear it.

Sure I do.

You'll think I'm being silly.

Then I definitely wanna hear it.

You don't want those you're venting *to* to think they're who you're mad *at*. Be clear who or what made you angry.

There was a choir singing Christmas carols at the mall.

And ...

I watched 'em and I got to thinking.

Come on, let it all out.

WHO DOES THE %#@ING CONDUCTOR THINK HE'S FOOLING?!

There. It's all out.

If you're going to vent, do it right. Get all of the anger out of your system, or else there's really no point.

He acts so important, but he's really just an inaccurate metronome! All he was doing was waving a stick around and making himself feel like a big man!

It's like he was playing with a tiny toy light saber.

No, that I'd respect.

Studies show that venting actually makes you angrier, and is pointless. Like many pointless things, it is really satisfying.

The choir isn't following him! The only hand motion he could make that'd make any difference would be to give them the finger.

That would affect their performance.

Yes, and I bet you the audience would applaud.

basicinstructions.net

It was Christmas. I saw a choir and their conductor. I genuinely got angry. He just looked so pleased with himself. When the choir was done singing, they stood motionless while he took a well-rehearsed bow. He's just lucky I didn't have a rotten tomato or he'd have gotten a gift.

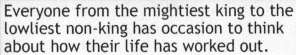

Everyone from the mightiest king to the lowliest non-king has occasion to think about how their life has worked out.

I never figured I'd be important or powerful, but thought I might at least work for someone important and powerful.

You work for me!

Yeah.

Think back to specific choices you made that could have drastically changed the direction your life took.

I considered becoming a minister.

Wow! That kinda changes my whole image of you.

Ministers make really good money.

And that changed it right back.

It's tempting to believe that if you had gone a different way you'd have been a success, but that's probably not true.

Wanting money is the exact wrong reason to become a minister.

How dare you force your idea of morality on me?

Do you even know what a minister is?

Yes, and I know you're not one.

And even if you would have succeeded, that might not be what's best for you, your loved ones, or the world.

I don't think ministers make much money.

That's just a matter of belief.

What, if you believe ministers make good money God will provide?

No, if the parishioners believe that ministers make good money, they'll pay me.

basicinstructions.net

How to Give Someone An Intangible Gift

by Scott MEYER

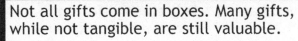

Not all gifts come in boxes. Many gifts, while not tangible, are still valuable.

An intangible gift might require some explanation for the recipient to fully understand its full importance.

You must be prepared for the fact that they may not fully appreciate your gift.

Rest assured, your gift's true value will be obvious to the recipient in time.

basicinstructions.net

41

BASIC INSTRUCTIONS

How to Explain Why You Haven't Put Someone in Your Comic Strip

by Scott MEYER

I know it's not a problem everyone faces, but we who do face it all the time.

If you haven't used someone in your comic, there's a reason. Just explain it as simply and diplomatically as you can.

Or just go ahead and put them in your comic. With some thought you should be able to come up with a way to use them.

It can be troublesome, but a little extra effort is a small price to pay for the pleasure of seeing their reaction.

basicinstructions.net

My older brother wanted to be in a comic.
My older brother signed a release.
My older brother does not ask to be in the comic anymore.

BASIC INSTRUCTIONS

How to Help Pick a Baby Name

by Scott MEYER

Most people eventually have children. Picking names is a popular way to involve their friends in the process.

My girlfriend's expecting!

You to marry her?

No, a baby! Wanna help me pick a name?

How about "Mary." I suspect your girlfriend will like the irony.

Naming a baby after a family member is a good way to honor the past and give the child an early sense of identity.

You could name it after your mom or dad.

Nah, we don't get along.

Grandparents?

No, they weren't good people.

Why are you reproducing, again?

To be a good parent and not make the mistakes they made.

You're off to a fine start.

They could name the child after someone who embodies the qualities they would have the child endeavor to possess.

I want a name that speaks of power and intelligence.

James? Kirk? Jean? Luke? Jean-Luc?

But not the name of a captain from Star Trek.

Hmmmmmmm.

Khan?

There are always "hip names" that will help a child fit in. They're a valid option, but try to avoid ones that are overused.

I like Jayden or Braeden, but they've been done to death.

How about "Burden"?

That's probably what society'll call your kid eventually anyway.

basicinstructions.net

BASIC INSTRUCTIONS
How to Select a Dish to Bring to an Office Potluck
by Scott MEYER

If your office has a potluck, it's common sense to bring a dish that you like.

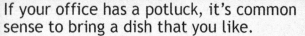

Have you decided what you're bringing to the potluck?

Yup! Brussels sprouts!

Aw. We don't deserve that.

It's funny. I agree with you, but for the exact opposite reason.

Most people aren't very adventurous. Bring something they're familiar with.

They're just tiny little cabbages.

Exactly! I like to eat them and pretend I'm a giant!

What kind of giant eats whole cabbages?

A vegetarian giant ...

who's too lazy to make cole slaw.

A potluck is a great opportunity to share new ingredients, cooking methods, or little known facts about the dish.

I hate brussel sprouts.

They're called "Brussels sprouts."

Yeah, Brussel sprouts.

Bru-ssels-sprouts.

Bru-ssel-sprouts.

Brussels sprouts.

Brussel sprouts.

You're saying it wrong.

I'M SAYING THE SAME THING YOU'RE SAYING!

YES, BUT WRONG!!

Remember, the point of a potluck is to create joy by sharing food you enjoy with the people you enjoy.

They're named after Brussels, Belgium.

Maybe. Or maybe they're named after the guy who discovered them.

Who's ever heard of a guy named "Brussel"?

Maybe he was named after Brussels.

THEN HIS NAME WOULD BE "BRUSSELS" AND WE'RE BACK WHERE WE STARTED!!

basicinstructions.net

I LOVE roasted Brussels sprouts. I never had them until fairly recently. Before that, every time I had them they'd been boiled to within an inch of their lives. It's as if our society didn't figure out how to cook or pronounce them until five years ago.

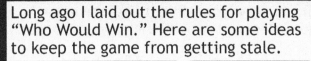

BASIC INSTRUCTIONS

How to Play "Who Would Win" (Advanced Techniques)

by Scott MEYER

Long ago I laid out the rules for playing "Who Would Win." Here are some ideas to keep the game from getting stale.

A Jedi who knows kung fu vs. a ninja who's strong in the force.

Stalemate. They'd just keep fighting forever.

That'd suck.

Yeah.

How long have we been playing "Who Would Win"?

Off and on, ten years.

Go obscure. Pick combatants who are less well-known, and theorize about the specifics of how the battle would work.

Sun Tzu vs. Machiavelli.

Sun Tzu at first, but Machiavelli would gain his trust then, in time, turn the tables on him.

Or they'd just write a book together that many middle managers would put on their desk, but never read.

Pick hypothetical contests other than the obvious war, fist fights, or sports.

Charles Nelson Reilly vs. Paul Lynde.

Interesting! How will they compete?

They don't! The question is, who'd be "top."

I won't dignify that with an answer.

You should be ashamed!

It's just so obviously Paul Lynde.

Take the winners of former games and pit them against each other, no matter how mismatched or nonsensical they are.

All right! Time for the big dance. Machiavelli vs. Paul Lynde.

Again, Paul Lynde. Again, only at first!

And this time they'd write a book many middle managers would read, but never put out on their desks.

basicinstructions.net

We all want to win, but defeat is a real possibility in any competitive endeavor.

Try to view your defeats as learning experiences that will make you stronger.

When it's clear you are being defeated, try to handle it as gracefully as you can.

The more you say right after a defeat, the more likely you are to say something you'll regret. Keep it short and pleasant.

© 2010: Scott Meyer

basicinstructions.net

BASIC INSTRUCTIONS — How to Express Yourself Forcefully — by Scott MEYER

People confuse expressing themselves forcefully with simply yelling, but they aren't the same thing at all.

FILL OUT THE RJ-17 FORM IMMEDIATELY!!

Okay.

WELL?!

You didn't say do it now. You said do it immediately. There's a big difference.

DO IT NOW!

Uh oh. Contradictory orders. Now I'm too confused to act.

Use of silence and lots of eye contact can get someone's attention far better than yelling ever could.

WHY'RE YOU STARING AT ME?!

Wouldn't you like to know?

YES! THAT'S WHY I ASKED!

When you do speak, choose your words carefully. The goal is to sound intelligent and serious, not angry and frantic.

Our mutual employer sent me with a message. He says to fill out the RJ-17 form right now.

Or what?

Or you'll face the harshest punishment he can imagine.

Which is?

My continued presence at your desk.

Remember, words are just an invitation. Actions are the party. What you do is far more important than what you say.

Fine. Stay. I don't mind.

Me neither. It's like a paid break for me!

What'd you do last night? I watched an old episode of Buck Rogers.

I'd forgotten how cool Twiki was.

BEEEDIBEDIBEDI BEDIBEDIBEDIBEDI

FINE!! I'LL FILL OUT THE FORM!! JUST LEAVE!

I've told this story before, but it bears repeating. I have stood in a room with one of the original Twiki costumes, and was infuriated when someone else misidentified the robot as Gort. What's happening to our educational system?

BASIC INSTRUCTIONS

How to Analyze a Corporation's Questionable Advertising Choices

by Scott MEYER

Every day we're surrounded by corporate advertising. It's no surprise that some of those ads seem wrongheaded.

> I saw a U-Haul truck the other day. On the side there was a cutesy cartoon U-Haul truck with a big, smiling face.

> Clearly they decided children weren't renting enough moving trucks.

If an ad confuses you, consider it from every angle to try to make sense of it.

> They've got the cartoon character. They might as well use it in TV commercials.

> "Watch your parents struggle to drive me!"

> "Sit in my cab and play guess what that stain-or-odor is!"

You might find that there's a good reason the ad was made the way it was.

> You realize that you're proposing a commercial where a cartoon character would eventually invite people to put their belongings in his butt.

Or, you may find that the ad is a mistake, and should've been made differently.

> Well, yeah!

> It'd be the most memorable ad EVER!

> "Sure that couch'll fit! There's plenty of room, in me!"

> "My extra wide rear door makes it easy to really pack things in!"

> "Is that leather? That's niiiice."

basicinstructions.net

How to Handle Exposition

by Scott MEYER

Exposition is background information the audience needs, but doesn't know. In the past, it was often handled by a narrator.

Evening finds the Knifeketeer hot on the trail of his lifelong arch-enemy, whom we've never heard of before this moment.

I didn't know you had an arch-enemy.

I don't like to talk about it.

Clearly!

It's often more elegant to have one of the characters explain the exposition to another character, and the audience.

His name is MacraMayhem. He has a black belt in the martial crafts.

How'd he get that?

I presume it involved knitting a black belt.

Once you get started, it's easy to end up endlessly explaining various plot points.

So we meet again! Uh, who's the kid?

That's my orphan sidekick, Stabby. His parents were found mysteriously murdered.

Stabbed?

How'd you know?

Lucky guess.

The most seamless method is to give the audience context clues, and let them figure things out for themselves.

I just found out MacraMayhem's been found dead, mysteriously stabbed eighteen times.

We might never know who did it.

You might not.

Drawings are like jokes. If you have to explain one, it wasn't any good. That said, the things sticking out of MacraMayhem's backpack are two giant knitting needles and a great big crochet hook.

BASIC INSTRUCTIONS

How to Get the Most Out of a Group Exercise

by Scott MEYER

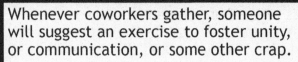

Whenever coworkers gather, someone will suggest an exercise to foster unity, or communication, or some other crap.

Hey! Wanna do something fun?

Yeah!

Let's do a team building exercise!

Sure. Before or after the fun?

If you're going to participate, you should do it right. Listen closely to the rules.

I say what I like least about the person to my left. Then they say what they don't like about the person to their left, and so on.

Then I start over with you?

Not likely. I'm making the rules. You say what you don't like about yourself.

Try to enter into the spirit of the thing. Participate to the best of your ability.

Graham has bad handwriting.

Athena's boss is a jerk.

Scott's boss sucks, so Scott retreats into science fiction rather than face it.

I have the same basic job as Salacious Crumb.

Afterward, discuss how the exercise went, and if you think it was effective.

That team building exercise was a huge success.

Everyone insulted me.

Nothing galvanizes a group like having a common enemy.

I'm not your enemy! I'm your leader!

There's less difference than you might think.

basicinstructions.net

Whenever you hear a sensational news story, you must first consider the source.

It seems our horoscopes have changed.

Eh, you can't believe everything you hear.

I heard it from a source I trust.

Yes, but I'm hearing it from you.

Another factor in the importance of a news item is how recent the report is.

It was on the news two weeks ago.

And of course you're bringing it up now. You never discuss anything until well after it happened.

You're like a time capsule.

Or a cartoonist.

If you're satisfied with the source and the freshness of the story, ask who it affects. You? Most people? Anybody?

But seriously! An imperceptible wobble in Earth's axis has thrown the astrological signs off by about a month.

I can see the headline. "Unimportant change changes something unimportant."

Once you're convinced that the story is worth the effort, dig into the details to see if the story stands up to scrutiny.

Aren't our signs supposed to determine our personality?

Yes.

And you say my sign has changed.

Yes.

Have you noticed a change in my personality?

You seem smugger. That might've been caused by the Zodiac's change.

Almost certainly.

basicinstructions.net

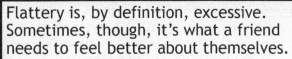

Flattery is, by definition, excessive. Sometimes, though, it's what a friend needs to feel better about themselves.

Sometimes I feel like a failure.

I'm surprised to hear that.

Really?!

Of course! "Sometimes."

It's been said that imitation is the sincerest form of flattery. Let your friend see you emulating their behavior.

Looka me. I'm Rick. Derp derp herp derp.

This isn't making me feel any better.

Mnis mninn'd mnaging mne mneel mnedder. Deeerrrrp.

Find something your friend genuinely does well, and compliment them on that.

You breathe well. Every time you inhale, you take in more oxygen than you need.

That's true! I'm a great provider ... of oxygen ... to myself.

Yes, and when you exhale, you selflessly share your hot, onion-scented surplus.

If your friend really needs a boost, often simply being present will help more than any deliberate attempt at flattery.

Please stop.

Have I helped?

As much as you're ever going to.

Well there's no need to thank me.

Agreed.

basicinstructions.net

BASIC INSTRUCTIONS

How to Compose a "Tweet"

by Scott MEYER

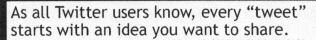

As all Twitter users know, every "tweet" starts with an idea you want to share.

Arthur C. Clarke once wrote that any sufficiently advanced technology is indistinguishable from magic.

Automatic paper towel dispensers must be advanced technology, 'cause I gotta wave my hands around like some kind of friggin' magician to ever make them work.

The idea then must be expressed in less than one hundred and forty characters.

So, will it fit in a tweet?

Almost, if I split it across two tweets.

So the answer is, "no," twice over.

The message can be shortened by using abbreviations and dropping words.

"Clarke said advanced tech like magic. Auto-paper towel machines must count, I must wave like magician to make work."

You sound like a caveman who has a friend named Clark.

Would it help if I add "LOL"?

Does it ever?

If it's still too long, try to reformulate the message to something that will fit.

"I appear to be invisible to all automatic bathroom fixtures. When the machines attack, I'll be like a filthy stealth bomber!"

Great. You've told the world you're a hygiene-challenged sci-fi nerd.

Yeah, I suppose it is old news.

I'll call my autobiography "Fighting Dirty."   basicinstructions.net

Few people love technology more than I do, but I've grown to hate high-tech public restroom fixtures. Motion-activated sinks, towel dispensers, urinals; all of them seem incapable of seeing me. If it weren't for the fact that I show up in the mirror, I'd suspect I was a vampire.

BASIC INSTRUCTIONS
How to Resurrect a Dead Character
by Scott MEYER

One of life's constants is that death is final. Science fiction is not like real life.

MacraMayhem's dead. I identified the body myself.

Hey everyone, MacraMayhem's robbing a bank downtown!

I identified him from a distance. I didn't wanna get too close to a dead body.

Some will explain away an inconvenient death using pseudo-science or magic.

Maybe he copied his brainwaves to a thumb drive, and rejuvenated his body in an occult ceremony.

Or maybe you got squeamish, passed out, and assumed he was dead.

NO! I saw his body ... BEFORE I passed out!

Others will think up a clever explanation why the character only seemed dead.

I used my martial crafts training to appear dead. You saw a false corpse I crafted from hot glue and Fimo clay.

But the way your lifeless eyes were rolling around in your head ...

Almost like craft store googly-eyes?

Exactly!

You can get away with resurrecting a dead character once or twice, but if you do it too often, you'll lose credibility.

Interfere with me in any way and Rodney dies ... again.

Please do as he says! I don't wanna die ... again.

Fine! You win this round ... again.

basicinstructions.net

BASIC INSTRUCTIONS
How to Capitalize on Your Talents
by Scott MEYER

We all have talents. In most of us, those talents are hidden beneath the surface.

Come on, Scott. If there's time to lean, there's time to clean.

I think you're underestimating how quickly I can lean.

Once you've identified your talents, you should try to use them in your work.

I'm a very fast leaner. It said so in my resume.

Oh. I'd thought that was a typo. So I guess you aren't a fast learner.

Neither of us is.

You will have to prove that you are talented, and that your talent is useful.

I'm not paying you to lean.

Well I'm not responsible for your questionable business decisions.

It's also important to understand your limitations, so you can play them down.

You'd get more bang for your buck paying me to lean than paying me to clean. I'm an extremely slow cleaner.

How slow?

I'm cleaning right now.

No, you're leaning.

And you can't spell "clean" without "lean."

basicinstructions.net

Synergy is when two things combine with beneficial results. Start with something that seems to serve little purpose.

> Some movies have an extra scene after the credits.

> Mainly superhero movies and dumb comedies.

> You're right. MOST movies have an extra scene.

Find a second thing that seems less than useful, but might be combined with the first thing in a creative way.

> And most movies have paid product placement.

> Not serious movies.

> Please! "The King's Speech" was like a two-hour-long commercial for tea.

The hard part is coming up with a creative way to combine your two items.

> In the next superhero movie, after the credits, the hero should stop the villain from stealing Hostess Fruit Pies.

> Hmmm, would Twinkie the Kid have a cameo?

> Why not? I'm sure Sam Elliott could use voice work.

Really successful synergy will often involve a third unforeseen factor.

> Comic book movies and junk food are advertised to kids. Your idea will only appeal to middle-aged guys who read comics.

> I like to call them "the young at heart."

> There's a big difference between being "young at heart," and having the mind of a child.

> Not from an advertising perspective.

*I haven't seen "The King's Speech,"

basicinstructions.net

I remember trying very hard to squeeze in a joke about how being "young at heart" was a figure of speech, and that most of the people we were talking about actually had the cardiovascular system of a much older person.

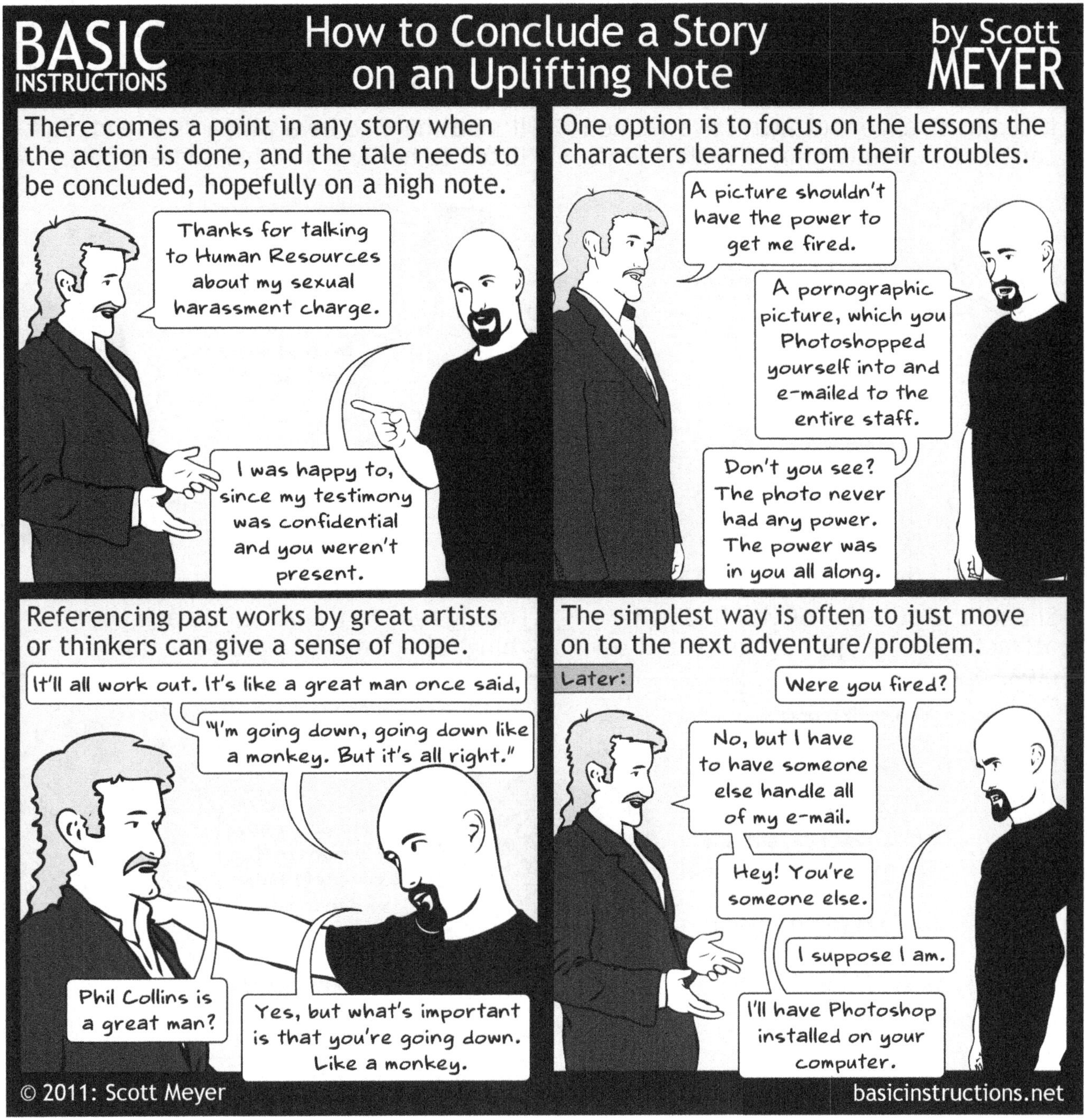
BASIC INSTRUCTIONS
How to Conclude a Story on an Uplifting Note
by Scott MEYER
There comes a point in any story when the action is done, and the tale needs to be concluded, hopefully on a high note.
Thanks for talking to Human Resources about my sexual harassment charge.
I was happy to, since my testimony was confidential and you weren't present.
One option is to focus on the lessons the characters learned from their troubles.
A picture shouldn't have the power to get me fired.
A pornographic picture, which you Photoshopped yourself into and e-mailed to the entire staff.
Don't you see? The photo never had any power. The power was in you all along.
Referencing past works by great artists or thinkers can give a sense of hope.
It'll all work out. It's like a great man once said,
"I'm going down, going down like a monkey. But it's all right."
Phil Collins is a great man?
Yes, but what's important is that you're going down. Like a monkey.
The simplest way is often to just move on to the next adventure/problem.
Later:
Were you fired?
No, but I have to have someone else handle all of my e-mail.
Hey! You're someone else.
I suppose I am.
I'll have Photoshop installed on your computer.
© 2011: Scott Meyer
basicinstructions.net

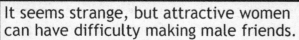

BASIC INSTRUCTIONS

How to Be Friends with an Attractive Woman when You're a Heterosexual Man

by Scott MEYER

It seems strange, but attractive women can have difficulty making male friends.

How're you?

Sensitive, with amazing stamina.

That's not really the answer I wanted.

Who knows what you women want?!

Not you.

It's not hard to be a woman's friend. Just listen to her and give her some credit.

So I said, "Not you."

Did you mean that he doesn't know what women want, or that women don't want him?

Which do you think?

Both.

Smart man.

Should the question of you finding her attractive come up, be honest, but set clear boundaries.

You're the only guy in the office who's never hit on me.

Well, you ARE very attractive, but not as attractive as the idea of remaining happily married and gainfully employed.

Again, smart man.

Having female friends can teach you things about men. Unpleasant things.

All I did was tell her about my stamina and sensitivity.

And in doing so, you demonstrated a complete lack of sensitivity.

That's why I really push the stamina angle by telling her often, and forcefully.

basicinstructions.net

When this comic first ran, there were those who asked why a man would want to be friends with a woman. Just asking that question shows that the person asking has a skewed definition of the word "friend," and the word "woman."

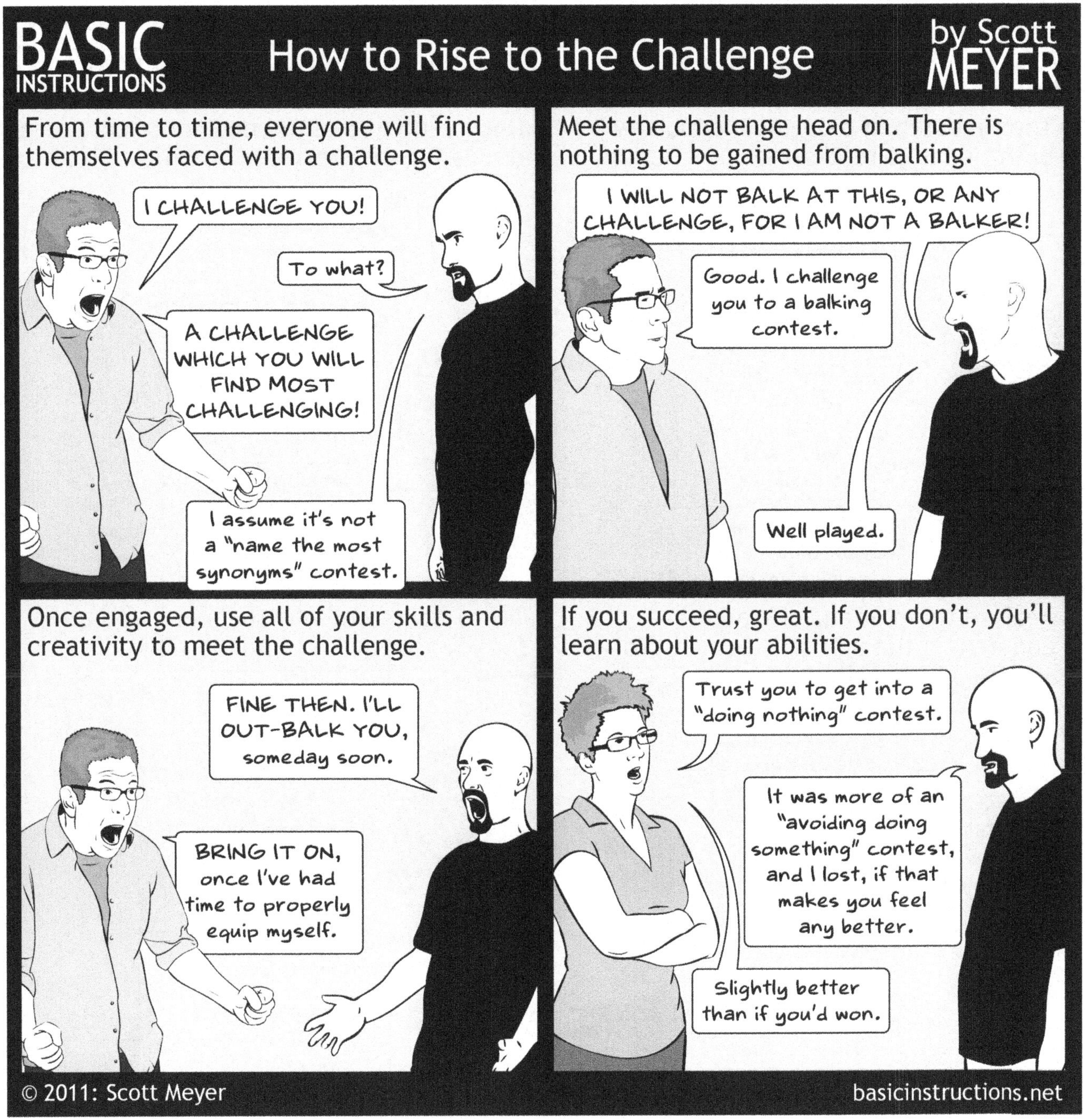
BASIC INSTRUCTIONS
How to Rise to the Challenge
by Scott MEYER
From time to time, everyone will find themselves faced with a challenge.
I CHALLENGE YOU!
To what?
A CHALLENGE WHICH YOU WILL FIND MOST CHALLENGING!
I assume it's not a "name the most synonyms" contest.
Meet the challenge head on. There is nothing to be gained from balking.
I WILL NOT BALK AT THIS, OR ANY CHALLENGE, FOR I AM NOT A BALKER!
Good. I challenge you to a balking contest.
Well played.
Once engaged, use all of your skills and creativity to meet the challenge.
FINE THEN. I'LL OUT-BALK YOU, someday soon.
BRING IT ON, once I've had time to properly equip myself.
If you succeed, great. If you don't, you'll learn about your abilities.
Trust you to get into a "doing nothing" contest.
It was more of an "avoiding doing something" contest, and I lost, if that makes you feel any better.
Slightly better than if you'd won.
© 2011: Scott Meyer
basicinstructions.net

The first step in enjoying a popular work of fiction is to read some good fiction.

I just finished reading "The Girl Who Kicked The Hornet's Nest."

So you've finished the whole trilogy.

Yup.

What was it all about?

Mostly about how no woman should ever go to Sweden.

Once you've read the book or books, discussing the story can be enjoyable.

Are you ever gonna read the books?

No.

So if I talk about them it won't ruin anything for you?

Just the next hour of my life.

Analyze the plot and characters. Try to understand the author's thought process.

They're about an anti-social woman who's super good at many things.

She befriends a middle-aged magazine writer who is totally irresistible to women.

The books were written by a middle-aged magazine writer, who, presumably, didn't date all that much.

Try to figure out why the story worked for you, so you can find more like it.

They're both super good at sex and violence.

Anything they're both not good at?

Maintaining stable relationships.

They're the perfect couple, from a literary point of view.

basicinstructions.net

BASIC INSTRUCTIONS
How to Increase a City's Tourism
by Scott MEYER

It may seem pointless, but if you have an idea to increase a city's tourist income, you should share it.

> Reno, Nevada turned down my proposal for a new slogan.

> They didn't like "Reno is for Clydes"?

> They said none of them knew what a Clyde was.

> What do you expect from a bunch of Clydes?!

Sometimes it's painfully obvious that the current methods just aren't working.

> What's their current slogan?

> "Reno: The biggest little city in the world."

> Accurate. Reno offers the crime of a big city with the crushing lack of opportunity of a small town.

It's not enough to dismiss the current plan. You must invent new ideas with which to replace it.

> "Reno: They'll never look for you here."

> "Reno: Come alone, with small, unmarked bills."

> "Reno: Come visit optimism's grave!"

When you have a solid idea, make your proposal. Sadly, it's not your decision to make, but you'll know you tried.

> I'm sending Reno my proposal for a new tourism slogan.

> "What happens in Vegas costs less in Reno."

> So, you're targeting thrifty adulterers.

> I prefer to call them "business travelers."

basicinstructions.net

Reno: Our slots are looser and our slogans are more suggestive! Reno: The Las Vegas of Laughlin! Reno: Come on Baby, don't be stuck up! Reno: Nobody can say they saw you here without admitting they were here themselves.

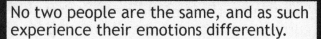

BASIC INSTRUCTIONS

How to Explore Your Emotions

by Scott MEYER

No two people are the same, and as such experience their emotions differently.

I've never been jealous. I don't know what it feels like.

How do you feel when someone else gets something you want but now cannot have?

Mad.

Well, you should feel jealous, if only of people who know what "jealous" means.

Discussing emotions with other people will help you understand them yourself.

I've realized there are only a few basic emotions, and the rest is just context.

So grief is just sadness, due to loss.

Yes.

And pride is happiness, due to the quality of your poetry.

Yes. And shame is sadness, due to the quality of your friend's poetry.

Another person's differing ideas about emotions may help inform your thinking.

Your theory is a nice start, but I can break down my feelings even further. I have identified two basic emotions.

Really?! Just two?!

Yes, "anger" and "not anger."

It used to be three emotions, but I eliminated "less anger."

It's uncomfortable, but being open about your feelings is productive and healthy.

Fear?

Anger.

Love?

Not anger.

I think you're on to something.

Your admiration makes me not angry.

basicinstructions.net

Prejudices are counterproductive and ugly. The sad fact is, we all have them.

Windows might be an okay operating system, but I can't use it. Bill Gates is such a jerk.

If you're gonna refuse to use a product because the founder of the company was a jerk, you're gonna have to stop using ...

products.

Prejudices are irrational. When one is confronted with logic, you can expect more irrationality will follow.

I have nothing against Apple, but you've gotta admit, Jobs was just as big a jerk as Gates.

THAT'S NOT TRUE!!

Come on. The man was clearly a jerk.

BUT I DO NOT HAVE TO ADMIT IT!!

Your best bet is to produce examples and evidence that gently prove your point.

If you won't use anything produced by a jerk, you can't drive a Ford, talk on a telephone, or use anything invented by Edison.

Edison?

The man used to electrocute animals.

Well science

As a marketing gimmick.

Yeesh! What a jerk.

If the person is at all reasonable, they'll eventually come around.

If it makes you feel better, they all had engineers doing the actual work.

Jerks seldom create stuff. They just seem to always get the credit.

That doesn't make me feel better.

Me either.

basicinstructions.net

Panel 1

One of life's most flattering and nerve wracking experiences is when someone asks you for constructive criticism.

Did you read my novel?

Yes.

How was it?

Predictable.

But did you enjoy it?

No. As I predicted.

Panel 2

If you're to be any help, you must be honest, even if the news is not good.

There was no suspense. I knew exactly what they were going to find in the shed.

Really?

The title of the book is "Blood Shed." It wasn't hard to figure out.

Panel 3

Once you've shared your opinions, give them a chance to defend their position. Who knows? They may change your mind.

Just because the book's called "Blood Shed" that doesn't mean the shed's gonna be full of blood. It could just mean someone's done a bunch of bleeding.

And where would they have done all this bleeding?

Okay. I see your point.

Panel 4

In the end, all you can do is tell them the truth. They'll either listen, or not.

It's nothing but people wondering what's in the shed till the last page, when they open the shed.

Then it says "It was blood! BLOOD!"

And that's the end.

I'm setting up the sequel. "Tears Shed."

You shouldn't write a book for the title.

I'm not. I'm writing it for the money.

Oh. That's okay then.

basicinstructions.net

BASIC INSTRUCTIONS   How to Unite Against a Common Foe   by Scott MEYER

It's a common plot device: two lifelong enemies being made to work together.

As you know, Rocket Hat, the Titanians' massive interstellar battle zeppelin is on its way here to our worlds.

I, as Emperor of the Moon, and you, as Earth's champion, have equal reason to stop them, for they mean to destroy the Moon ...

likely singeing parts of Earth in the process.

The two parties will be evenly matched, but with different skills and weaknesses.

I shall do what I do best.

Give a rambling, threat-laden speech.

And you will do what you do best.

Prevail.

There's more to it than that.

Sorry. Prevail, through an act of horrifying violence.

Devise a plan that capitalizes on each party's strengths and specialties.

We shall meet with the Titanians. You in chains, me holding your leash.

I shall offer you to them in exchange for peace. If they refuse, you will attack.

If they accept, I'm cool with that.

It's vital to have a plan, but it's also important to be flexible, and work together as a cohesive unit.

Rocket Hat saved the day!

I helped.

Yes, Sire! You helped, by dangling helplessly from the leash and acting as a wrecking ball.

The Titanians were utterly helpless.

Indeed! They were laughing too hard to dodge.

    basicinstructions.net

The Titanians are from Saturn's moon Titan. They resent the moon men for calling themselves "the Moon Men" when Titan is a much larger moon. I've put more thought into the backstory for the Titanians than I have for the characters I actually show in the comic!

BASIC INSTRUCTIONS

How to Introduce a "New" Superhero

by Scott MEYER

Introducing new heroes with similar powers to older ones is a practice as old as Superman himself. Ask Captain Marvel.

Hello, Omnipresent Man.

Who the %$#* are you?

I'm Mister Everywhere!

Oh. Go away.

Not likely.

Subtle changes between the original and the new character are the key to making the new hero more than a mere copy.

I'm an exciting new superhero with powers that are, coincidentally, similar to yours.

How similar?

Identical.

That's pretty similar.

Of course, if both characters exist in the same narrative universe, they will almost certainly be at odds with each other.

NGAAH! What are you doing here?!

Same thing I'm doing everywhere.

You're not just everywhere. You're everywhere with me, and that's a problem, because I work alone.

So do I, next to you.

If both characters fight for the side of good, they must eventually learn to coexist peacefully.

Look, I need some privacy.

Fine, I'll turn my back.

You're still looking at me.

From two different angles!

NGAAAAAAAAAAAAAAAHHHHH!!!!

basicinstructions.net

I've written myself into a corner. Omnipresent Man is everywhere. Mr. Everywhere is too, and I've established that my superheroes don't die. Now I can't put Omnipresent Man in a comic without Mr. Everywhere unless it's a prequel, which only occurred to me just now.

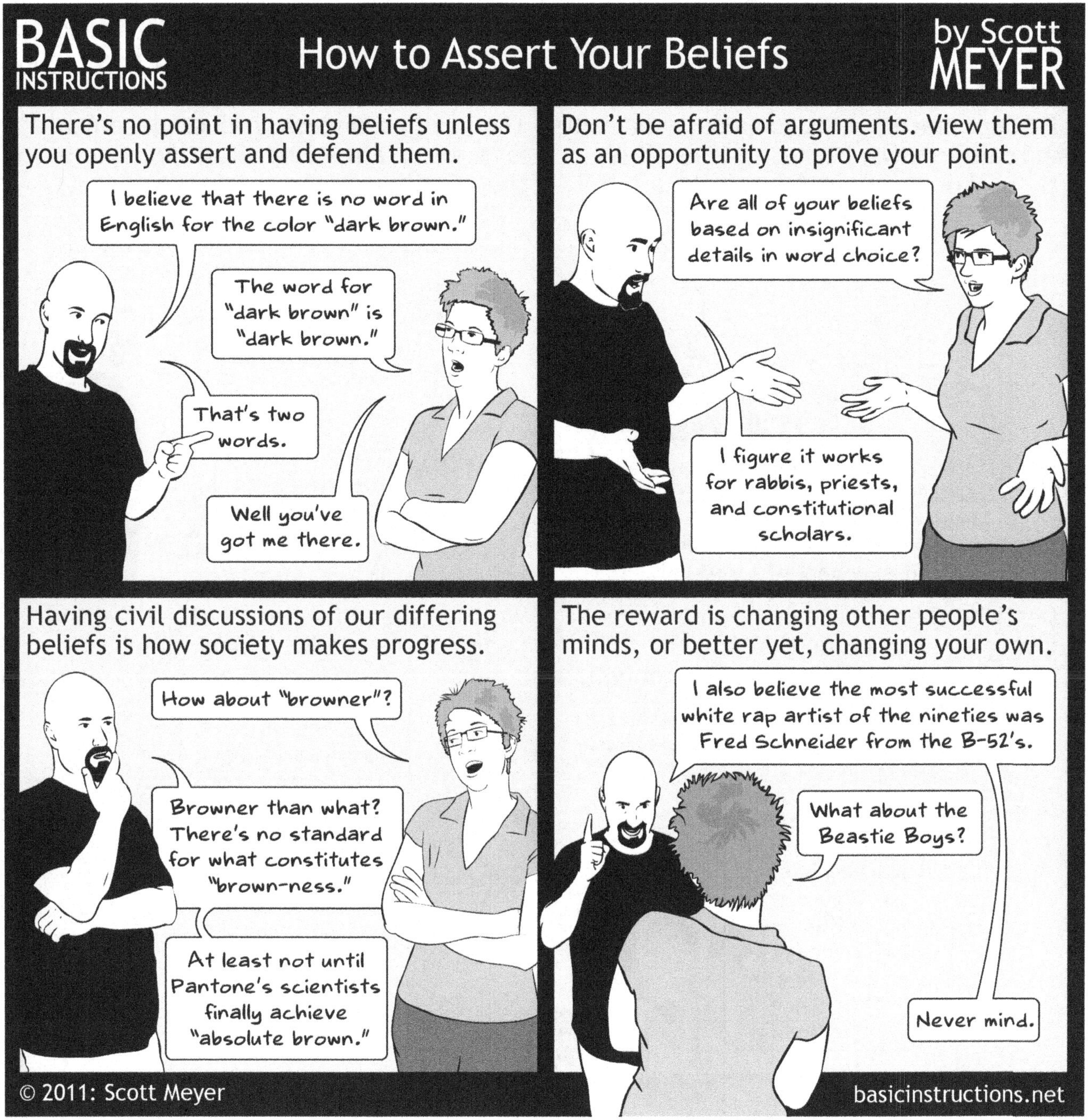
BASIC INSTRUCTIONS
How to Assert Your Beliefs
by Scott MEYER
There's no point in having beliefs unless you openly assert and defend them.
I believe that there is no word in English for the color "dark brown."
The word for "dark brown" is "dark brown."
That's two words.
Well you've got me there.
Don't be afraid of arguments. View them as an opportunity to prove your point.
Are all of your beliefs based on insignificant details in word choice?
I figure it works for rabbis, priests, and constitutional scholars.
Having civil discussions of our differing beliefs is how society makes progress.
How about "browner"?
Browner than what? There's no standard for what constitutes "brown-ness."
At least not until Pantone's scientists finally achieve "absolute brown."
The reward is changing other people's minds, or better yet, changing your own.
I also believe the most successful white rap artist of the nineties was Fred Schneider from the B-52's.
What about the Beastie Boys?
Never mind.
© 2011: Scott Meyer
basicinstructions.net

Panel 1:

Product placement is common, especially in reality shows, because the reality is that TV producers need to make a profit.

Does The Biggest Loser really expect us to believe that Ziploc bags are a diet aid?

They expect us to think making a morbidly obese person cry on camera is a legitimate part of a workout.

Panel 2:

The key to seamless product placement is to set up a realistic situation, where there's a believable problem to solve.

I'm depressed.

Of course you are!

I might feel better if I talked about it.

You might.

A good friend would ask me what's wrong.

Probably.

Panel 3:

Describe the product in glowing terms, giving the impression that it is the easiest solution to this, or any problem.

You know what makes me feel better? My Bose noise-canceling headphones!

They deliver full, rich sound while blocking out any irritating noises like traffic noise, airplane engines, or you listing the reasons you're depressed.

Panel 4:

Wrap up the placement with a lingering image of the product doing its job.

SO GO ON AND TELL ME WHAT'S BOTHERING YOU.

For starters, my best friend is a complete...

SAY, WOULD IT HELP CHEER YOU UP IF I PLAYED AIR GUITAR?

basicinstructions.net

It doesn't matter how good you think a song or band is, someone will disagree.

What are you listening to?!

It's a band from the '70s called "The Guess Who."

NO TIME! NO TIME! NO TIME! NO TIME! NO TIME! NO TIME! NO TIME!

"Guess who." My guess is it's angry hippies.

The person criticizing your tastes likely listens to things you don't like either.

I like this band. Don't mock them!

You mock Duran Duran all the time!

I criticize Duran Duran. There's a difference.

You said "The Reflex" triggers your gag reflex.

A valid criticism!

No matter how strongly you feel, it's important to remain rational and civil.

I rarely say anything bad about Duran Duran.

You insult them at least once a day, every day.

But if you look at it as a subset of times I'd like to insult them, that's a very small percentage.

In the end, musical tastes are subjective and cannot be quantified or explained.

It's not that I don't like Duran Duran. It's just that I prefer other bands.

Like who?

What do you mean?

You said you prefer other bands.

Yes. I prefer other bands. All other bands.

basicinstructions.net

"The Guess Who" is not a good name. Their Wikipedia page makes for surprisingly interesting reading. Turns out the name was foisted on them after a poorly thought-out marketing ploy. Before that they were called "Chad Allen and the Expressions," which is an even worse name.

BASIC INSTRUCTIONS
How to Use Deductive Reasoning
by Scott MEYER

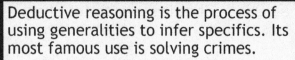

Deductive reasoning is the process of using generalities to infer specifics. Its most famous use is solving crimes.

My cell phone was stolen.

Stolen, eh? Clearly, this is the work of ...

Criminals.

That narrows it down.

First, gather as much information about the problem at hand as you possibly can.

Where was it stolen? / Dunno.

When? / Sometime before now.

What kind of phone was it?

A metallic pink Motorola RAZR.

And you want to find the person who took it. / Yes.

To thank them?

Use the information you have gathered to make educated assumptions.

Your phone was taken by someone who would want a pink RAZR.

Meaning the phone was taken by you, or a thirteen year old girl.

There has to be another option.

Could've been you AND a thirteen year old girl. I doubt you could pull this off on your own.

Your conclusions may be surprising, but if your facts are correct and your logic is sound, be confident in your answer.

Got my phone back. I'd just misplaced it.

Did you, or did you hide it from yourself?

That's ridiculous.

Is it, or is it brilliant?

I'm hanging up.

Are you, or ...

Okay. I guess you are.

basicinstructions.net

The first step in comparison shopping is to go out and see what's available.

NGAH! What's wrong with that movie?! Was it shot with a camcorder?

New TVs do that. They call it "Motion Smoothing."

I call it "Mexican Soap Opera Mode."

Once you know what you want, go online and read some actual customer reviews.

Amazon's customers give that TV three stars overall. Most gave it five stars, but some gave it one.

They can't both be right.

Agreed. So I have to figure out who's stupid, the majority or the minority.

Ask people you know for their opinions. They will often have new insights.

I have one of those! I wrote a review for it on Amazon. Gave it one star.

Good to know.

Once you've bought the item, you'll be happy that you did your homework.

We should turn on "Mexican Soap Opera Mode" and watch a Mexican soap opera.

No. The TV might overload and go up in a "bola de fuego"!

basicinstructions.net

"Motion Smoothing" simulates the look of filming at a higher frame rate, thus looking more realistic and showing more detail. Most people's first reaction is to say that it looks worse, not better. The fact that "more realistic" means "worse" is kinda telling.

BASIC INSTRUCTIONS

How to Be a Good Husband During "Ladytimes"

by Scott MEYER

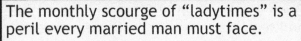

The monthly scourge of "ladytimes" is a peril every married man must face.

The ladytimes are upon me.

As always, I'll help in any way I can.

As always, there's nothing you can do.

As always, that's why I'm so quick to offer.

The primary hardship for a husband is watching his wife suffer through a problem he'll never really understand.

I imagine it must be awful.

For you to really understand, one day a month I'd have to kick you in the nuts repeatedly.

That's your answer for everything.

Should an opportunity to ease your wife's suffering present itself, jump on it.

I do have a way you can help.

I'd be proud to.

I need you to go to the store.

I'll start assembling a disguise.

If you're sent out for "supplies," don't try to act manly to compensate. Nothing is manlier than being a good husband.

Did you know that these are excellent for dressing gunshot wounds?

No, I didn't. Please tell me more! It'll pass the time 'til security gets here.

basicinstructions.net

I am a considerate husband. I will go to the store to get my wife feminine hygiene products whenever she asks. Missy is a considerate wife. She never asks me to go buy her feminine hygiene products. EVER!

Reality repeats itself, and patterns are everywhere. Many are quite surprising.

What's that they're making?

A hot tub.

I'd have sworn it was some kinda boat.

If you think about it, boats and hot tubs do the same thing.

They waste money.

Natural patterns often tend to be subtle. Man-made patterns are more obvious.

I do enjoy watching "How it's Made."

Actually, this is "Factory Made."

What's the difference?

"Factory Made" is on later, and makes money for a different producer.

Often, upon noticing a pattern, it will seem incongruous and out of place.

The music is ... I dunno. What do you call upbeat instrumental music that was clearly made by one guy with a keyboard?

Porno music.

Yes. This music is porno music.

Upon further examination, seemingly random repetitions may turn out to be part of a much larger pattern.

The whole show is cheesy music and tight close-ups of mindless automatons joylessly performing repetitive tasks.

They've applied the techniques of the porn industry to educational TV.

And we've watched five straight episodes.

basicinstructions.net

BASIC INSTRUCTIONS

How to Understand Men's Fashion

by Scott MEYER

There are three basic strategies that men use when choosing clothes. One is to choose lots of sports team logo wear.

Do you really have to wear a Seattle Mariners shirt and Seattle Mariners sweat pants too?

Yes. That's the whole point! If the team logos match, the clothes match.

It's like Garanimals for men.

A more timeless approach is to dress more formally, relying heavily on suits.

You should pay a little more attention to your wardrobe. Buy some suits!

Yeah!

The pants and jacket are the same material. They can't not go together!

He did say "a little" more attention.

Some men will develop a personal uniform, selecting a look they like and varying it little from day to day.

Do you own anything but black t-shirts?

I own shirts in many colors.

Dark charcoal. Ultra-dark blue. X-treeme gray.

Your closet must look like a rainbow, re-imagined by Tim Burton.

No matter what method he chooses, a man's goal when selecting his ensemble is always the same.

You're all pathetic!

But we're pathetic on our own terms.

So you're deliberately failing and calling it strength of character. What kind of way to live is that?

The manly way.

basicinstructions.net

Sports team apparel. Superhero T-shirts. Suits. Dockers. Cowboys. Bikers. Emos and goths. Construction workers. Cops. All four branches of the military. One way or the other, most of us men show our individuality by picking which uniform we'll wear. There's something to that.

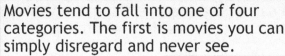

BASIC INSTRUCTIONS
How to Decide Whether to Rent, Buy, or See a Movie in the Theater
by Scott MEYER

Movies tend to fall into one of four categories. The first is movies you can simply disregard and never see.

Netflix has that new Meryl Streep movie.

What's it about?

Her sleeping with Alec Baldwin.

What a waste of a great actress.

Well, they needed her to seem to enjoy it.

There are movies that you think you might like to see, but care little about. These are the movies you rent.

There's a new Jason Statham movie. He plays a driver who beats people up.

How's that different from any of his other movies?

I haven't seen this one yet.

Some movies, due to their scope, your interest, or your wish to vote with your dollars, must be seen in the theater.

I should see Suckerpunch on the big screen.

What is it?

Beautiful women, huge explosions, and violence.

But what's the story?

Once upon a time there were beautiful women who perpetrated violence, then exploded. The end.

If a movie holds some deep personal meaning for you, or you will watch it repeatedly, consider buying a copy.

I hate Big Trouble in Little China!

It's got everything. Spectacle, violence, beautiful women! I saw it when I was a kid and it totally shaped my taste in movies.

That's why I hate it.

basicinstructions.net

When someone has surprising news, they may try to get you to guess what it is.

Guess who has a date?

A woman with low standards.

Yes, but guess who else?

You can help the querent surprise you by guessing exactly as they would expect.

The angry client's coming in. Guess how many of us are meeting with him?

All of us.

Lower.

Three of us. You, me, and the client.

Lower. The answer is "two." It's just you and him.

That's pretty low.

You could guess the opposite of how they expect, deliberately messing them up.

What do you think the odds are of me going to this meeting of yours?

Hmm, about twenty percent.

Well I ... uh. I thought you'd say one hundred percent.

Sorry, I wasn't listening. I was trying to decide how much to cut your pay if you don't go.

If possible, don't guess at all. Answer the question with a direct statement of fact.

How long do you think I'm gonna keep coming in here and being disappointed?

Until you wise up and fire us.

That's not the answer I was hoping for.

So I've disappointed you. Never saw that coming.

basicinstructions.net

BASIC INSTRUCTIONS

How to Curse with Flair

by Scott MEYER

People curse to express their feelings forcefully. Ironically, nothing is less forceful than incompetent cursing.

> YOU'RE FULL OF %#@&! YOUR BOSS IS FULL OF %#@&! YOUR WHOLE COMPANY'S A PILE OF %#@&! I'M SO SICK OF THIS!

> Sick of this %#@&?

> %#@& YEAH!

One way to make your curses memorable is to employ some wit and originality.

> I don't suppose you happen to rent donkeys, do you?

> What? NO! Why would you ask me that?

> BECAUSE I AM ABOUT TO GO TO TOWN ON YOUR @$&!!

Express your ideas as directly as you can, using occasional profanity like a garnish.

> We are kinda like %#@&. Not actual %#@&. The word.

> Because, even though we never get you results you keep using us over and over. Just like you keep repeating the word "%#@&" like a parrot.

> A %#@&-parrot, if you will.

The most memorable way to curse is to express a strong, genuine emotion.

> I must say, that was, by far, the lamest %#@& I've ever heard.

> Yes, YOU must.

Most people only curse when they're upset. Upset people don't choose their words well, so we often end up with poor quality cursing. Incompetent cursing can be funnier than the good stuff. One time a kid called my dad a "boob-butt-brain." We still laugh about it, years later.

BASIC INSTRUCTIONS
How to Avoid a False Bargain
by Scott MEYER

Many apparent bargains aren't worth even the modest amount they cost.

I got my girl some perfume for her birthday.

Good stuff?

Eh, it's not bad.

Well I'm sure she'll be not unappreciative.

When evaluating a possible purchase, do not let optimism cloud your judgement.

I went to the perfume outlet and got a deal on a bottle marked "factory second."

You bought her irregular perfume?

You can barely smell the difference.

Does it say that on the bottle?

No, but I wrote it in the card.

Don't be dazzled by perceived savings. Be skeptical of limited time offers, free gifts, and oversized portions.

It came in a bottle the size of a mayonnaise jar.

Is it an old mayonnaise jar?

That's just silly. It's a perfume jar.

Now.

An item that is useless is a waste of money, no matter how little it costs.

I don't care how cheap it was, if it doesn't do its job, it's a waste of money.

It's perfume. Its job is to smell good.

No, it's a gift.

Its job is to make your girlfriend happy.

Oh. I'd better buy her something else.

Perhaps some factory refurbished chocolates.

basicinstructions.net

BASIC INSTRUCTIONS

How to Handle Shocking News of a Highly Personal Nature

by Scott MEYER

Occasionally we learn unfortunate things about people we thought we knew well.

Ugh. I forgot to take my meds this morning.

Oh! I'm sorry. I didn't know.

That there's something wrong with me?

No, I knew that. I didn't know you were seeking treatment.

Don't dig for details, but listen if they are offered. Remember, it is a great honor for someone to confide in you.

I'm sorry. It must be difficult.

It can be. I suffer a malady that's often misunderstood.

Chronic dry eye.

I certainly misunderstood.

You can't really know what it's like to have their problems, but try to imagine.

We victims of chronic dry eye get no sympathy, because people can't tell how upset it makes us.

For all you know, I'm crying right now.

You're not.

I COULD BE!!

Things affect everybody differently, so show some sympathy, even if others' problems seem inconsequential to you.

Where's our telethon? Where are our bracelets? Maybe we could have a yellow visor or something.

You're right! You're being marginalized! Who cries for the dry-eyes?!

Nobody! And we need it more than anyone!

basicinstructions.net

BASIC INSTRUCTIONS

How to Wish Your Friend a Happy 50th Birthday

by Scott MEYER

Be sensitive to your friend's wishes. They may not want the fact that they are turning 50 to be common knowledge.

I'm writing a comic about a friend turning 50, but I know you're sensitive about it, so I'm going to take steps to hide your identity.

Thanks. That's very kind of you.

You're welcome, Rick.

If your friend seems to be taking their birthday badly, remind them that they have a lot to be proud of.

I always saw myself as the live fast, die young, leave a good-looking corpse type.

But Rick, you've created your own unique lifestyle.

Live slow, die old, leave a crowd of angry creditors.

If they're still depressed, make sure they know that it's normal to feel that way.

I know exactly how you feel. I'll be turning 40 soon. It's a hard pill to swallow.

Yes, I remember what that was like.

A decade ago.

You were so old then.

Remember, it's their birthday. Celebrate it the way they want to, or not at all.

How do you plan to celebrate?

The way I celebrate every major milestone.

I'm gonna hide somewhere and pretend it isn't happening.

Every day's a celebration.

basicinstructions.net

BASIC INSTRUCTIONS

How to Act When You Meet a Celebrity

by Scott MEYER

Unexpectedly meeting a celebrity can be jarring, and may put you off balance.

Celebrities are just people. They most likely don't want you to make a big deal about them, so try to be cool.

Try not to read too much into the words and actions of a celebrity. It will only make your meeting more awkward.

Later, when telling your friends about your brush with fame, the classy move is to be as complimentary as you can.

© 2011: Scott Meyer

basicinstructions.net

I wrote this after meeting a famous woman I respect deeply. I did not expect to find myself speaking to her and I mumbled like a moron. She was gracious, which made it worse. My only consolation is that she has the fond memory of the time she was kind to an idiot.

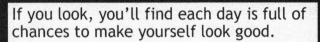

BASIC INSTRUCTIONS — How to Enhance Your Reputation — by Scott MEYER

If you look, you'll find each day is full of chances to make yourself look good.

There's a 5k charity run next month. I put a sign-up sheet for sponsors in the break room.

So, if we donate money, you'll do something pointless and unpleasant.

It's a good cause, the money goes to

I don't need more convincing.

By helping others you look generous, thereby helping yourself in the process.

I see you donated ten bucks for Graham's charity run.

Maybe. He only collects if he gets over two hundred dollars in pledges.

So, you've bet ten bucks that everyone else is stingy.

Seems like a safe bet.

Of course, any deliberate attempt to look good can have the opposite result.

Even if he does make it, everyone'll see my name at the top of the donation sheet for the next month.

That explains why you printed your name in huge letters with a glitter pen.

I paid ten bucks for an ad that says I'm a generous person.

Or a ten year old girl.

Everyone's perception is different and unpredictable. Try to do the right thing and your reputation will build itself.

I told everyone your plan, so you don't look generous anymore.

Nope! Now I look clever.

If by clever you mean conniving and sneaky.

And I do.

basicinstructions.net

BASIC INSTRUCTIONS

How to Create a Diversion

by Scott MEYER

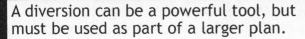

A diversion can be a powerful tool, but must be used as part of a larger plan.

Part one of our plan was to capture you, Rocket Hat, the only Earth-Man who has ever bested us.

No other Earth-Man has ever dared to resist us.

They've never had to.

When designing your diversion, take into account your adversary's interests.

For decades we have watched you simpletons, and we have deduced what Earth-Men find most diverting.

Sex, impossible computer generated action sequences, and a confounding game called foot-ball, which is played differently depending on where you live.

Make your diversion something that will completely enthrall your adversary.

We have prepared a digital simulation of the Chicagoed-Bears playing Manchester United while wearing giant robot suits.

But what of the sex, Sire?

We shall have the one who resembles my Moon-Empress wear something "slinky."

The one called "Madden"?

Indeed!

Once your diversion is in play, capitalize on your advantage without hesitation.

Rocket Hat escaped while we were contemplating a scantily clad Madden.

Our diversion was so powerful it diverted us!

A diversion this powerful must be kept secret.

Meaning?

If you tell anyone of this, I will kill you.

basicinstructions.net

I spent an embarrassing amount of time playing around with catchy names to call "a scantily clad Madden." A "Scladden"? A "Scantily Maddily"? I think I ended with a "Scad-ladden." It's a diversion so powerful it actually diverted me from the act of describing it.

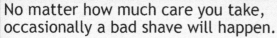

BASIC INSTRUCTIONS
How to Recover from a Bad Shave
by Scott MEYER

No matter how much care you take, occasionally a bad shave will happen.

I have shaved. It did not go well.

You should be more careful.

I couldn't be more careful. I went over it five times.

Small though they are, the cuts on your face should still be treated as wounds.

I have stuck toilet paper to my face, because that is what one does.

It covers the cuts and stops the bleeding, right?

That too, but mainly it makes the whole experience so degrading that you'll be less likely to ever do it again.

Be careful not to let blood from your shaving wounds stain your shirt collar.

What's with the paper towels?

They keep me from bleeding on my shirt.

Interesting technique.

It was invented by Shakespeare.

Your cuts will heal on their own, if you give them time and leave them alone.

Have you stopped shaving your neck?

Just until it heals, or I have a magnificent neck beard.

I think the cuts are preferable to a neck beard.

You're not the one getting cut.

You're not the one looking at a neck beard.

basicinstructions.net

BASIC INSTRUCTIONS

How to Run a Joke into the Ground

by Scott MEYER

First come up with a joke that is equal parts funny, silly, and annoying.

Baaaabadap dopdopdopp dop dop

What is that?

The best rock song ever written.

Baaaabadop baDOP DOP

I thought it was the theme from Magnum P.I.

Glad you recognized it!

Repeat the joke as often as possible until everyone is tired of it but you.

BADADA BA BA, BAA BAA BA DOMP DOMP

That's not funny anymore.

So you admit it was funny at one time.

Sorry. I misspoke. That's still not funny.

Then I've got nothing to lose. BADADA BOMPBOMP BOMPBOMP BADUMP

Take a brief break from the joke, then do it again. It will be substantially funnier.

ba ba BA BOMP!

If you're gonna answer the phone that way, just let me go to voicemail.

DONE! I think you'll enjoy my new outgoing message.

Really?

No, but I know I will.

Repeat the previous steps. Each time you resurrect the joke it will be funnier.

In the event of his demise, Scott asked that we play the following video at his funeral.

Thank you all for coming.

Ahem.

Baaaabadap dopdopdopp dop dop

basicinstructions.net

It's hard to convey an instrumental song in words, but that works to my advantage here in two ways. It makes the whole thing seem more ridiculous, and if you could actually hear the theme to Magnum P.I., you'd be too distracted by the awesomeness to finish the comic.

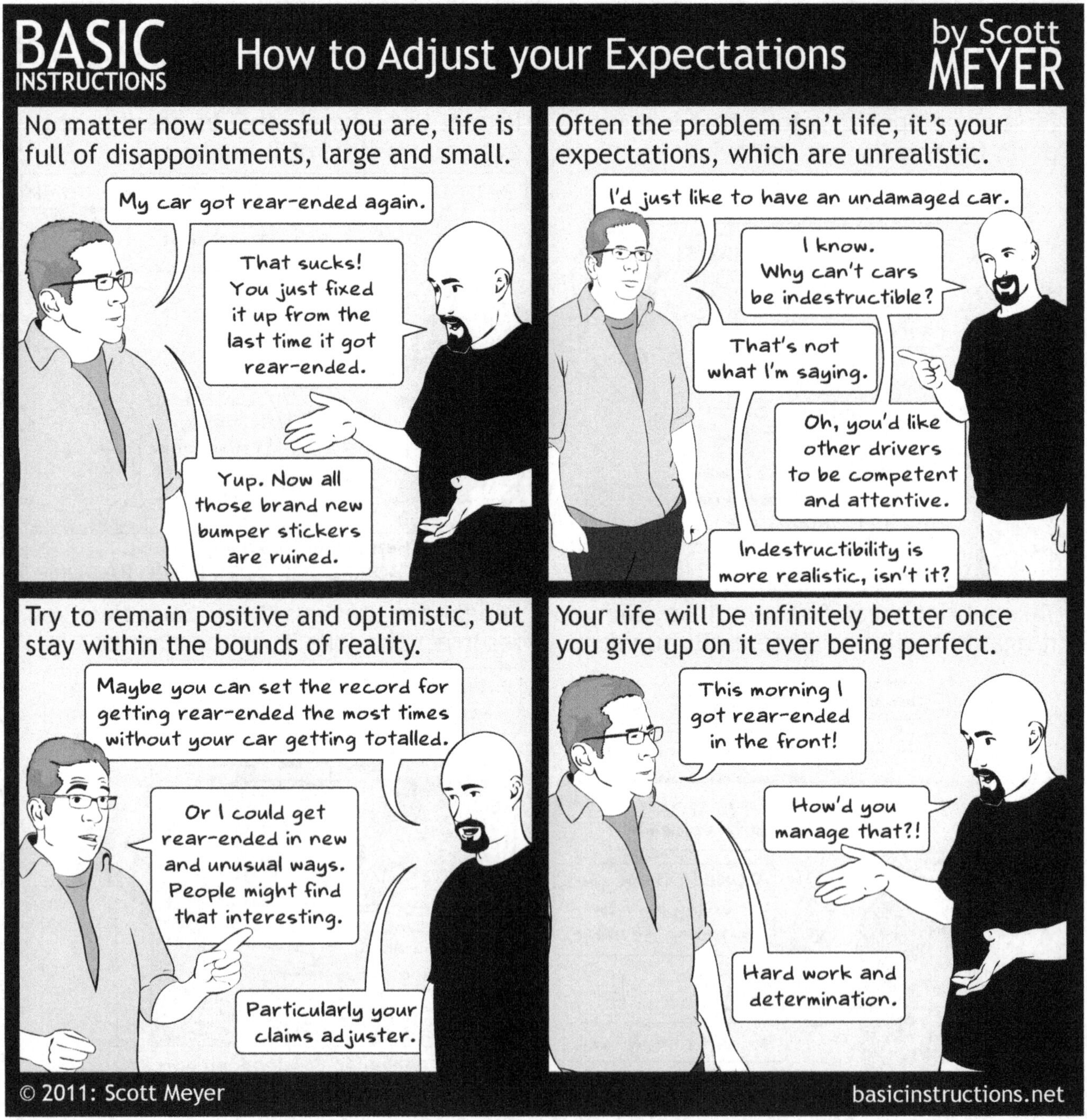
BASIC INSTRUCTIONS
How to Adjust your Expectations
by Scott MEYER
No matter how successful you are, life is full of disappointments, large and small.
My car got rear-ended again.
That sucks! You just fixed it up from the last time it got rear-ended.
Yup. Now all those brand new bumper stickers are ruined.
Often the problem isn't life, it's your expectations, which are unrealistic.
I'd just like to have an undamaged car.
I know. Why can't cars be indestructible?
That's not what I'm saying.
Oh, you'd like other drivers to be competent and attentive.
Indestructibility is more realistic, isn't it?
Try to remain positive and optimistic, but stay within the bounds of reality.
Maybe you can set the record for getting rear-ended the most times without your car getting totalled.
Or I could get rear-ended in new and unusual ways. People might find that interesting.
Particularly your claims adjuster.
Your life will be infinitely better once you give up on it ever being perfect.
This morning I got rear-ended in the front!
How'd you manage that?!
Hard work and determination.
© 2011: Scott Meyer
basicinstructions.net

BASIC INSTRUCTIONS

How to Learn from Other People's Mistakes

by Scott MEYER

Panel 1

You can learn much from other people's mistakes. As such, people who make lots of mistakes can be valuable friends.

I'm getting married.

For real this time?

I guess. Do you have any advice about planning a wedding? You've both been married.

I'm still married.

Yeah, but I've been married more times, to many different women, so pipe down, newbie.

Panel 2

Ask your friends about their experiences. Focus on their ideas that did not work.

Once I wrote a poem and read it before the vows. I still get asked to recite it occasionally.

Wow! It must've really been something!

It was called "She and Me Make We." And yes, it really was "something."

Panel 3

Once the failed ideas start flowing, don't do anything that might stop them.

Your tux should be just as grand as her dress.

Mine had ruffles, a jewel-encrusted cummerbund, and tails so long they needed a bearer.

Yeah, I guess I was honored to be part of the wedding party, but still ...

Panel 4

You'll find that some people are mistake factories. Often, they're the people most confident in their own wisdom.

And didn't she leave you at the altar for upstaging her wedding dress?

Just as well. Who wants to be married to a prima donna like that?

© 2011: Scott Meyer

basicinstructions.net

My wife and I were married in Vegas by a civil servant at City Hall. My innovative ideas for how a wedding ceremony should be staged might have led Missy to suggest the ceremony we had. To this day my go-to wedding gift is matching his-and-hers Nerf guns.

BASIC INSTRUCTIONS

How to Assert Your Intellectual Superiority

by Scott MEYER

Anybody in a position of authority will at some point have to demonstrate why they are the one making the decisions.

Why are you always the one making the plans?

The superiosity of my skills, which are far too numerous to list now.

But which include word invention and point evasion.

Address the doubters, making it clear that they are not the first to doubt you, and that previous doubters were wrong.

There have always been doubters. At the university they called me mad!

You went to a trade school.

Well, at the trade school they called me mad.

You tried to weld wood.

Admit to previous mistakes, but point out any factors that led to your failure.

I lacked the proper tools. I was unprepared.

Of course they didn't have the tools for woodworking. It was a broadcasting school!

So you admit broadcasting school left me unprepared!

It's broadcasting school. That's what it does!

Be persistent. The intelligence of your arguments will grow more undeniable with each new point of logic you raise.

You fools can't begin to understand the brilliance of my schemes!

You should devise a brilliant scheme to explain your schemes.

No, we'd get caught in an endless explanation loop.

How so?

Here, I'll explain.

basicinstructions.net

I went to radio broadcasting school. My instructor told us the industry was dying and that we should choose something else. When I graduated I learned that many program directors don't hire broadcasting school graduates. When I did get a job, I found I hated it. Money well spent!

Proper use of language can elevate the discussion of even the most base topic.

I propose we attend a film that has an unbalanced female-to-male ratio.

Which gender would enjoy a majority?

The females.

How would this female majority be clad?

In a word, "scantily."

Capital!

The ability to communicate well is a valuable skill, and can also be a burden.

Why do I always have to talk to the angry clients?

Because you talk good.

I think you mean that I talk well. I'm not helping myself, am I?

You can't help yourself.

It's more than just vocabulary and proper grammar. There are certain words and phrases that seem to scream "classy."

It is, as always, indescribable to see you.

Indescribably unpleasant?

Oh, I shouldn't say that.

But you would.

Indubitably.

The ability to communicate well should be used to share the truth, not hide it.

So your coworkers have been procrastinating.

Oh heavens no! If anything, they've been malingering.

A procrastinator intends to do something, eventually.

basicinstructions.net

Sometimes you get a feeling or thought you don't want to say, but that you can't get off your mind, so you say nothing.

You're quiet lately.

Oh. Yeah. Sorry.

That wasn't necessarily a complaint.

The only way you'll ever banish the thought is to find someone you can talk to and tell them what's on your mind.

I don't wanna talk about it.

Oh come on.

I've been thinking and, uh ...

Yes.

I just can't respect any man with a comb-over.

I can see why you didn't want to talk about it.

There's no point in expressing half of a thought. Be bold. Don't mince words.

When a man has a comb-over, he's saying that he thinks everyone else is dumb enough to be fooled by a little creative combing!

It's like wearing an "I'm with stupid" shirt with a drawing of a hand pointing at the reader!

Which has been done. I looked into it!

Note: what you say may offend people. That's why you hesitated to begin with.

Furthermore, a comb-over tells the world: "This person has something about himself he doesn't think either he or society can accept."

A comb-over is a tiny little closet you wear on your head for all to see.

There, I said it.

And you never have to say it again.

But I could NEVER EVER.

Yes, I did write this comic with Donald Trump in mind.   basicinstructions.net

I mean every word of this comic! When a man has a comb-over it either means that he's dumb enough to think it looks convincing, or he thinks the rest of us are dumber than him and will think it looks convincing. Neither of those is a good thing.

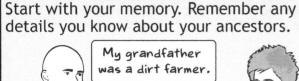

BASIC INSTRUCTIONS

How to Find Your Roots

by Scott MEYER

Start with your memory. Remember any details you know about your ancestors.

My grandfather was a dirt farmer.

How does one make a decent living dirt farming?

I said he was a "dirt farmer," not a "decent living maker."

Delve into the details, not just of their lives, but also their place and time.

My other grandfather made moonshine.

Oh! Was he involved in car racing?

You're thinking of southern 'shine runners. He was a northwestern moonshiner.

What did they do?

They drank.

Don't get caught up in dates and titles. Try to see your ancestors for who they were as human beings.

But he had a lot of kids, right? Surely that shows that he had a lot of love in him.

Yes, he had a deep, abiding love for free child labor.

The internet has many resources that can offer information about your family tree.

I've found a photo of the prison where my maternal great-great-grandfather was sent for killing a man over stolen beer.

Also, it seems in WWI, the Germans made mustard gas by a process they called "The Meyer Method."

It turns out most of the things you could call "surprising" are "surprisingly bad."

basicinstructions.net

Panel 1

Like many unpleasant things, political disagreements pop up unexpectedly and cause discomfort and embarrassment.

See CSI last night?

NO I DID NOT!

We should all get back to work NOW!

I've never heard you suggest that we all get back to work.

You've never discussed CSI with Jenkins either.

Panel 2

When faced with a disagreement, lay out your position as clearly as possible.

Police shows are biased and offensive.

How so?

I'll ask you. Who always turns out to be the bad guy?

The murderer?

THAT'S RIGHT! THE MURDERER!!

Panel 3

Don't deal in abstractions. Make them see the human face of the problem.

Do murderers always have to be the villains?

YES! THEY'RE MURDERERS!

I bet if I brought a murderer in here you'd change your tune in a hurry.

OH GOD!! PLEASE DON'T!!

See?! You're happy to do some murderer-bashing unless a murderer's in the room.

Panel 4

At the base, all political change happens one mind at a time, but real results come when many people work together.

Some day, the murderers will organize.

Awesome. A "Million Murderer March."

YES! And then they'll get some attention.

I BET!

basicinstructions.net

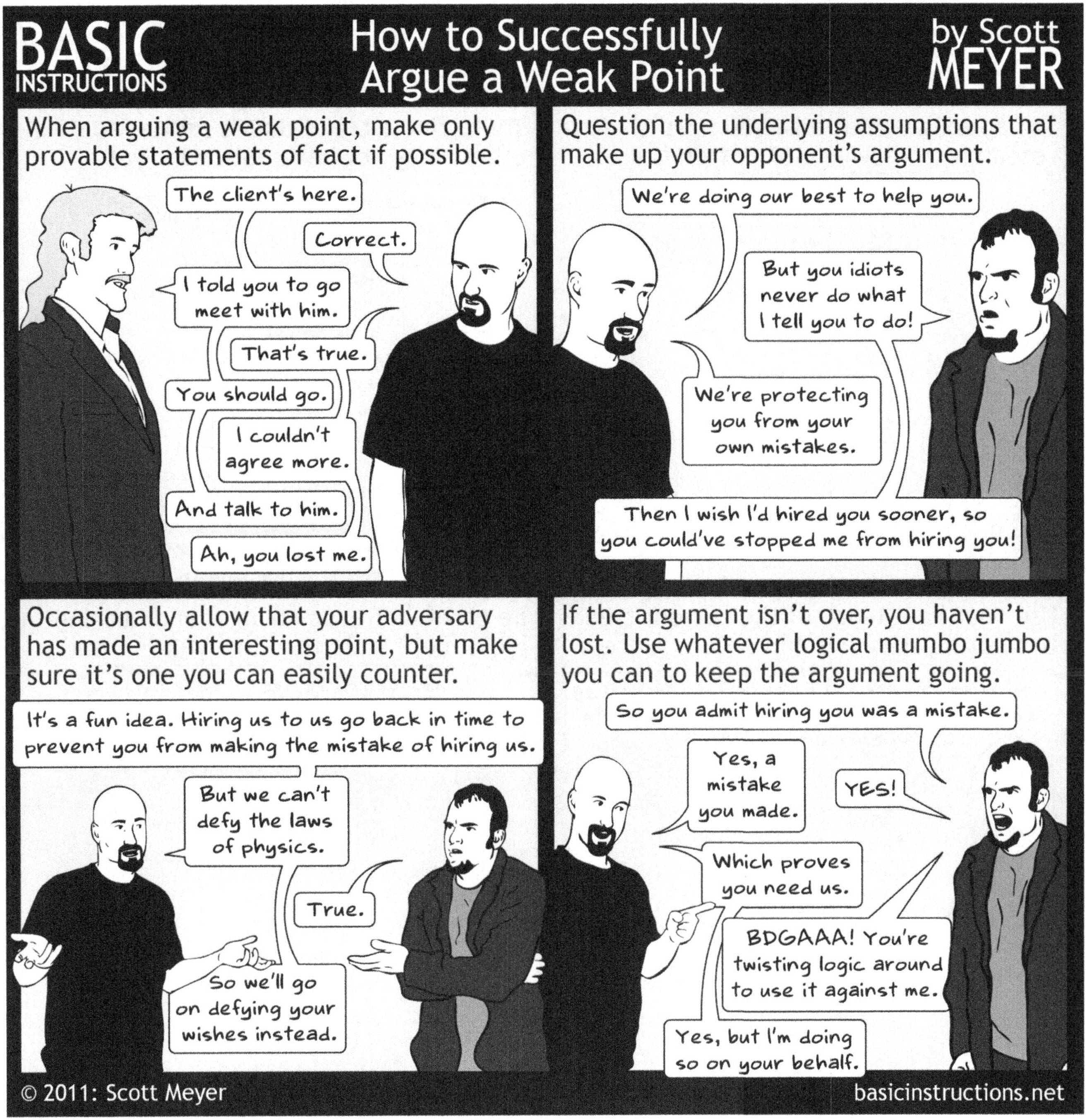
BASIC INSTRUCTIONS
How to Successfully Argue a Weak Point
by Scott MEYER
When arguing a weak point, make only provable statements of fact if possible.
The client's here.
Correct.
I told you to go meet with him.
That's true.
You should go.
I couldn't agree more.
And talk to him.
Ah, you lost me.
Question the underlying assumptions that make up your opponent's argument.
We're doing our best to help you.
But you idiots never do what I tell you to do!
We're protecting you from your own mistakes.
Then I wish I'd hired you sooner, so you could've stopped me from hiring you!
Occasionally allow that your adversary has made an interesting point, but make sure it's one you can easily counter.
It's a fun idea. Hiring us to us go back in time to prevent you from making the mistake of hiring us.
But we can't defy the laws of physics.
True.
So we'll go on defying your wishes instead.
If the argument isn't over, you haven't lost. Use whatever logical mumbo jumbo you can to keep the argument going.
So you admit hiring you was a mistake.
Yes, a mistake you made.
YES!
Which proves you need us.
BDGAAA! You're twisting logic around to use it against me.
Yes, but I'm doing so on your behalf.
© 2011: Scott Meyer
basicinstructions.net

BASIC INSTRUCTIONS

How to Capitalize on Current Trends

by Scott MEYER

To capitalize on trends, you need to do research to know what the trends are.

I've been researching TV shows.

Watching TV.

Well, Jane Goodall "watched" chimps.

Yes, but she wasn't sitting on a couch eating chips.

So I planned better than her. Sue me.

Try to find a trend that is subtle, so that others may not have noticed it yet.

TV cops don't solve crimes anymore.

Who does?

Pathologists, mathematicians, body language experts, writers, neurosurgeons, and at least one serial killer.

What do the cops do?

They alternate between fighting the hero and thanking them.

Use your knowledge of the current trends to inform your plans and ensure success.

Poker players are hot right now, so I'm writing a show about a gambler who solves crimes to win a wager with the Mayor.

THAT'S NOT BAD! What's it called? "Dead Man's Hand"?

I was thinking "Murder, I Bet," but that's much better.

Be careful. Trends change, and nothing looks more stale than last year's trend.

Or how about "I'll See ... Your Corpse!"

Poker's passé. Now it's all about guys who buy abandoned storage lockers.

REALLY?! CRIPES!! What happened to our standards?

They died, and their belongings were sold at auction to a guy in a tank top.

basicinstructions.net

Reminiscing often just happens when talking to people with whom you shared your childhood, like friends or siblings.

Remember that Christmas we got the Green Machines?

Yeah, that was awesome.

I didn't get one.

It was really awesome.

Should an old argument or grudge come up, briefly acknowledge it and move on.

Really, only I got a Green Machine.

'Cause that's what you asked for.

You got the same basic thing, but in black with Batman logos, so yours was much cooler.

'Cause that's what I asked for. "Same thing as him, but much cooler." That's what I always asked for.

Try to keep the mood light by focusing on the good times and the happy memories.

We'd race around the driveway.

Yeah, that was fun. You'd yell at me to slow down. I'd yell at you to keep up.

I'd cry because you wouldn't let me have a turn.

It was really fun.

Reminiscing helps us remember with more clarity and greater perspective.

Then dad said he was going to make the driveway better.

He covered it with four inches of loose gravel, making it totally impossible to pedal anything.

Good times!

basicinstructions.net

That Batman-themed Green Machine is probably one of the coolest things I ever owned. It was black and yellow, with Batman logos and a flag on the back. Later on, I found that the fiberglass flag pole made a pretty effective weapon. It was truly the gift that kept on giving!

Ancient and unspeakable evils are often trapped in innocent-looking artifacts.

Check out this weird book I bought. It's bound in rough, scaly leather.

It's strangely warm to the touch, and it emits a distant hissing noise.

Publishers'll do anything to get your attention these days.

If an artifact houses an evil force, avoid it unless you have a compelling reason.

"Serpens Simiae Sinestra."

I admit, the title's not much of a "grabber."

"Foreword by Stephen King."

And that's why I bought it.

I admit, that man can really write a foreword.

Releasing the evil that dwells within an artifact requires complex preparations.

I'm gonna go home, draw a bath, light some candles, and do some reading.

Say, does your bathroom still have that weird pentagram motif?

You buy a condo from goths, you take what you get.

It was nice of them to give you the goat-blood scented bath bomb as a housewarming gift.

Once you've released the ancient evil, try your best to keep it in check.

Well done. You've unleashed the Snake-Ape.

Luckily, it saw me naked in the bath, and is paralyzed with embarrassment.

Or maybe pity.

EMBARRASSMENT!

basicinstructions.net

When I made up the Snake-Ape, I was trying to think of the stupidest monster of all time. Now, reading it again, my first thought was that if I wrote up a treatment and pitched it, Syfy might just commission a screenplay.

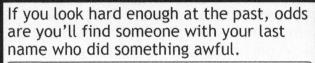

If you look hard enough at the past, odds are you'll find someone with your last name who did something awful.

So, in WWI, the Germans used a process called "The Meyer Method" to make mustard gas. I bet that kinda bothers you.

You know me too well.

I also bet when "Meyer Method" popped up on Google, you were hoping it was a sexual technique.

Far too well.

Logically, you're not responsible for the actions of dead people you never met.

Well I looked him up, and Viktor Meyer did a lot of really important, impressive stuff.

Really?

Yeah! So I figure the odds of him being related to you are pretty remote.

And if you look hard enough you may find that they weren't evil, but flawed and misguided, as most of us are at times.

And even if he was related, he probably didn't set out to create a horrible chemical weapon.

It was mustard gas!

Well yeah, but if he was related to you, he was most likely trying to invent an inhalable condiment.

In the end, you can't change the past. You just have to deal with the present.

We Meyers do enjoy some mustard on our bratwursts.

Maybe THAT'S "The Meyer Method."

IT'S NOT A SEXUAL TECHNIQUE!!

And it never will be if you don't try.

basicinstructions.net

BASIC INSTRUCTIONS

How to Get Into Your Opponent's Head

by Scott MEYER

To "get in their head" is to make your opponent spend time thinking about what you'll do, not of what they'll do.

I should warn you, I plan to get in your head.

When do you plan to start?

Perhaps I already have.

No, you haven't.

Then ... soon.

Be unpredictable. If they don't know what you're going to do, they can't plan a response. Keep them guessing.

Why are you holding that kitchen knife?

So I can use it later.

Maybe I'd feel better if I knew what you were going to use it for.

Offensive purposes.

Hmm. Okay. I don't feel any better.

Once they realize they can't predict your actions, your opponent will waste all of their energy trying to do just that.

Offensive purposes?!

That might mean he'll attack me. Or he might do something morally offensive with it.

Either way, I should at least get a decent story out of this, so that's something.

When you act, your move must be effective, or all this effort is wasted.

That's it? You stabbed my hotel?!

YEAH!! WHAT'LL YOU DO NOW?!

Charge you rent. I can charge for a damaged hotel. You've stayed at a motel. You know that.

basicinstructions.net

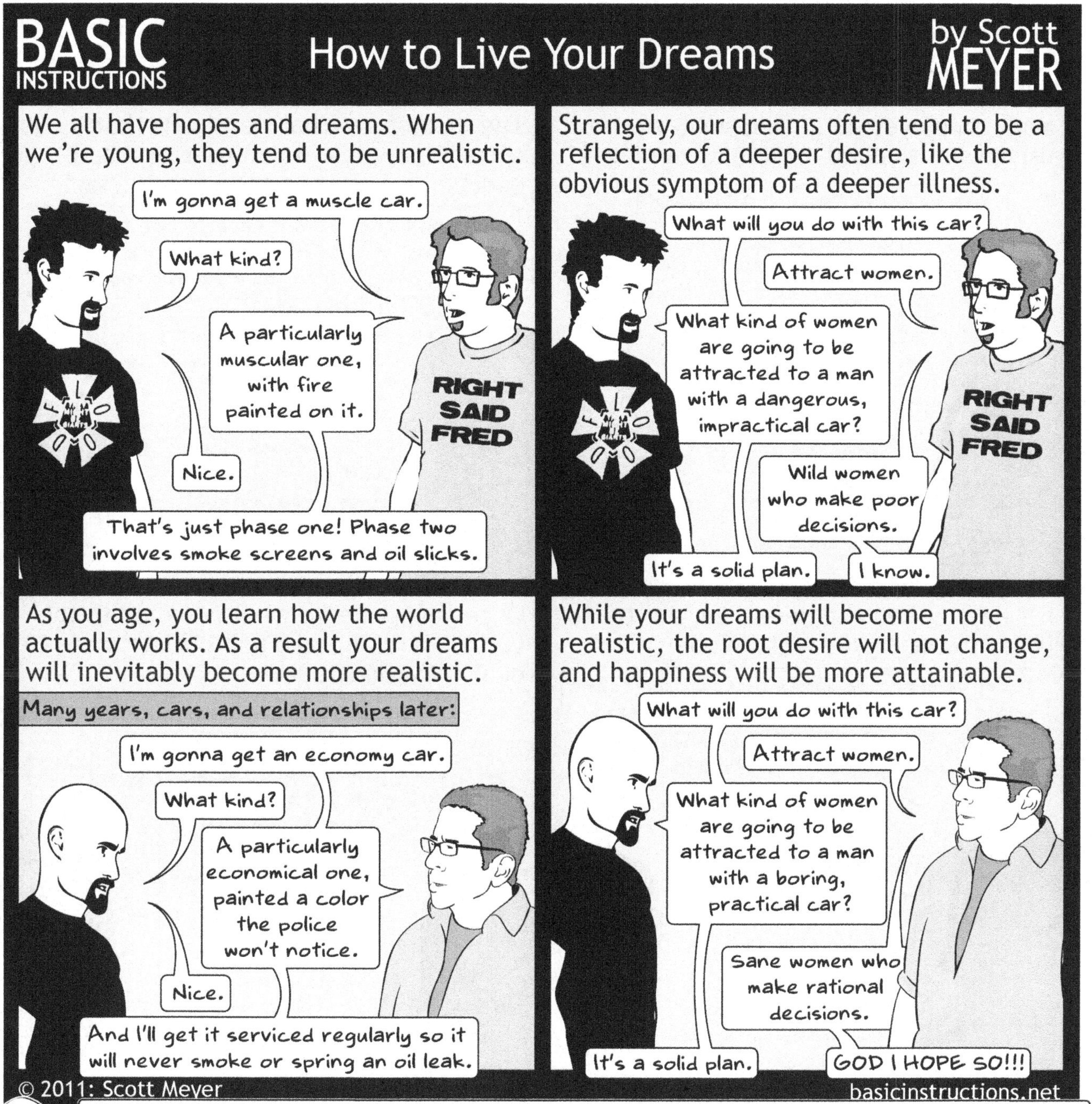
BASIC INSTRUCTIONS
How to Live Your Dreams
by Scott MEYER
We all have hopes and dreams. When we're young, they tend to be unrealistic.
I'm gonna get a muscle car.
What kind?
A particularly muscular one, with fire painted on it.
Nice.
That's just phase one! Phase two involves smoke screens and oil slicks.
RIGHT SAID FRED
Strangely, our dreams often tend to be a reflection of a deeper desire, like the obvious symptom of a deeper illness.
What will you do with this car?
Attract women.
What kind of women are going to be attracted to a man with a dangerous, impractical car?
Wild women who make poor decisions.
It's a solid plan.
I know.
RIGHT SAID FRED
As you age, you learn how the world actually works. As a result your dreams will inevitably become more realistic.
Many years, cars, and relationships later:
I'm gonna get an economy car.
What kind?
A particularly economical one, painted a color the police won't notice.
Nice.
And I'll get it serviced regularly so it will never smoke or spring an oil leak.
While your dreams will become more realistic, the root desire will not change, and happiness will be more attainable.
What will you do with this car?
Attract women.
What kind of women are going to be attracted to a man with a boring, practical car?
Sane women who make rational decisions.
It's a solid plan.
GOD I HOPE SO!!!
© 2011: Scott Meyer
basicinstructions.net

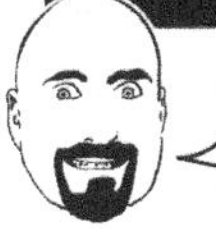

When I first moved to Seattle I had a 1962 Ford Fairlane. Seattle has steep hills and small parking spaces. The Fairlane had a three-speed transmission and a trunk the size of a dinner table. Eventually I had to choose between the car or Seattle.

BASIC INSTRUCTIONS
How to React to A Verbal Warning
by Scott MEYER

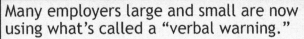

Many employers large and small are now using what's called a "verbal warning."

We need to talk.

AGREED!

There's a ton of stuff messed up around here, and you're responsible

Let me rephrase.

You need to listen.

The idea of a verbal warning is that it corrects a problem before it gets bad enough to warrant more formal action.

Look, I'd rather not have to talk to you about this, but it's important that we fix this before I have to give you a written reprimand.

I type up the written reprimands.

You can see why I want to avoid asking you to do one for yourself. I mean, how awkward is that?!

It's easy to become defensive, but try to listen to their issue with an open mind.

There've been complaints that you don't take instruction well, and that you don't listen.

I can see why you chose to give me a verbal warning.

I'm glad you understand!

Apparently, another problem with me is that my sarcasm is too subtle.

Once you've heard what issue led to the verbal warning, take appropriate steps to deal with the situation.

So, who complained about me?

If I told you, you'd go yell at them, and that'd discourage them, or anyone else, from coming to me with their complaints in the future, and that would be unfair ...

To Jenkins.

basicinstructions.net

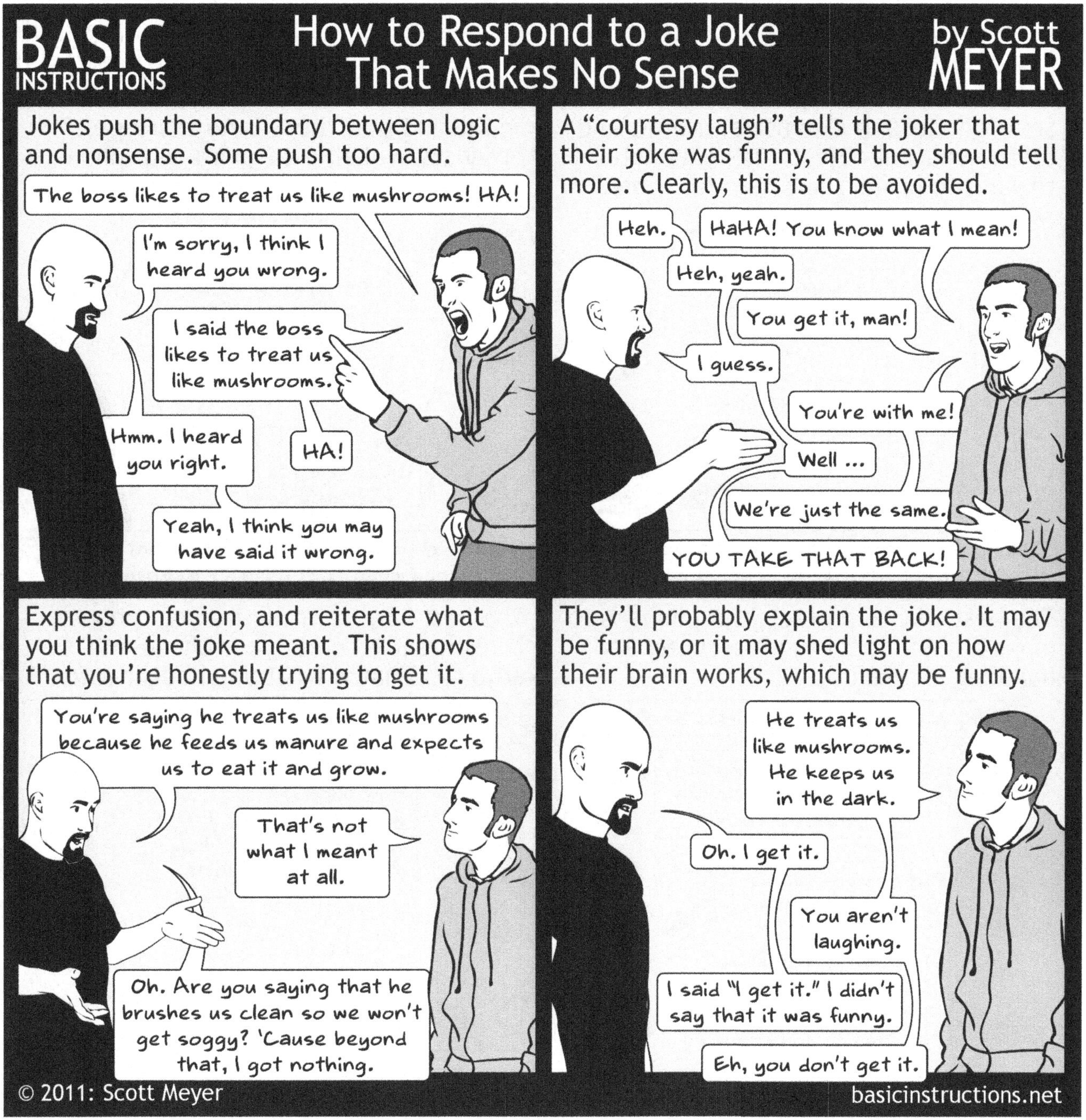
BASIC INSTRUCTIONS
How to Respond to a Joke That Makes No Sense
by Scott MEYER
Jokes push the boundary between logic and nonsense. Some push too hard.
The boss likes to treat us like mushrooms! HA!
I'm sorry, I think I heard you wrong.
I said the boss likes to treat us like mushrooms.
HA!
Hmm. I heard you right.
Yeah, I think you may have said it wrong.
A "courtesy laugh" tells the joker that their joke was funny, and they should tell more. Clearly, this is to be avoided.
Heh.
HaHA! You know what I mean!
Heh, yeah.
You get it, man!
I guess.
You're with me!
Well ...
We're just the same.
YOU TAKE THAT BACK!
Express confusion, and reiterate what you think the joke meant. This shows that you're honestly trying to get it.
You're saying he treats us like mushrooms because he feeds us manure and expects us to eat it and grow.
That's not what I meant at all.
Oh. Are you saying that he brushes us clean so we won't get soggy? 'Cause beyond that, I got nothing.
They'll probably explain the joke. It may be funny, or it may shed light on how their brain works, which may be funny.
He treats us like mushrooms. He keeps us in the dark.
Oh. I get it.
You aren't laughing.
I said "I get it." I didn't say that it was funny.
Eh, you don't get it.
© 2011: Scott Meyer
basicinstructions.net

Smartphones are expensive, useful, and often beautiful objects. It's only natural to want to protect and care for them.

> Got my new phone!

> That's a huge screen!

> It's super-durable, smudge-resistant high-tech glass.

> Is it responsive?

> Dunno. I ain't touching it 'til I get the screen protector I bought for fifty cents on Amazon.

You'll find that there is no shortage of products available to guard your phone.

> Where's your new super-sexy phone?

> This is it. I bought this protective case to keep it looking good forever.

> But you can't see it because it's in a huge ugly case.

> Think of it as a time capsule that'll be opened when I get a bigger memory card.

The best way to protect your phone is to make a habit of storing it securely and handling it carefully.

> Why is your phone in a Ziploc bag?

> It makes it waterproof, and I can still use the touchscreen.

> But can you talk on it through the bag?

> How'm I gonna talk underwater? No, when submerged it's strictly texting and e-mail.

The best way to maximize your phone investment is to use your phone and enjoy it. That is what you bought it for.

> 2 Years Later:

> Time to get a new phone, and my old phone still looks great!

> How much can you sell it for?

> Nothing. It's badly outdated.

> So it's garbage.

> Yes, but it's mint-condition garbage.

basicinstructions.net

BASIC INSTRUCTIONS — How to Talk to Someone Who's Lucky
by Scott MEYER

Panel 1

Penn Jillette said, "Luck is probability taken personally." Most of us live with a roughly equal mix of good and bad luck.

You're lucky you have a job.

Yes, but I'm unlucky that it's this job.

You're lucky I know you're joking.

Am I?

Are you what? Lucky or joking?

Does it really matter?

Panel 2

There are people who seem to have more good luck than others. Those people will often deny luck played any part at all.

I don't need luck. I started with nothing and made myself.

You bought a thriving business, floundered for years, then sold it to a corporation that hasn't fired you because they can't without incurring a contractual penalty.

Yes, but before all that, I had nothing.

Panel 3

Show them the things for which they should be grateful, but don't expect that this will make them grateful to you.

You didn't have nothing! You had a ton of money!

Nope. Inherited it the day I bought this dump. Before that everything was in my mom's name.

Imagine what that was like. A grown man still driving my mom's car.

Your mom's Corvette.

Mom had taste.

Panel 4

If being lucky doesn't make them feel lucky, odds are your words won't either.

Ya know, luck's like a big ugly moustache. People who have it don't notice it, and people who don't have it have trouble focusing on anything else.

I don't see your point.

Which is, in fact, my point.

*Several readers have pointed out he was

In case you've wondered, yes, I do see the irony of me insulting Mullet Boss's moustache when my only distinguishing characteristic is a chin beard that is as emblematic of the '90s as his moustache is of the '70s. It's like I walk around with a Pearl Jam concert on my face.

BASIC INSTRUCTIONS

How to Face Certain Death

by Scott MEYER

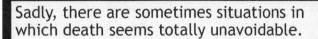

Sadly, there are sometimes situations in which death seems totally unavoidable.

ROCKET HAT! We shall do battle, sealed inside my Imperial Pummeltorium. Just you and me and a variety of pointy weapons.

The weapons will be evenly distributed.

In a large sack.

Held by me.

How you face certain death will be remembered by the people around you.

I'm about to be sealed into the Pummeltorium with Rocket Hat.

Promise me that no matter what happens, how scared I sound, or what you hear, PROMISE ...

That you'll open the door and save me.

Even in the face of certain failure, it's important to craft a plan for success.

I must devise a plan that plays to my strengths.

I suggest dodging as long as you can. Then you shift into cringing.

Standard procedure.

Indeed, Sire. Then after you've cringed, hit him with the shrieking.

He'll be confused because he'll be expecting my usual piteous weeping.

If you should survive, you'll be able to look back on your actions with pride.

I'm proud to say I never gave up.

Yes, Sire! You kept dodging no matter how still he stood, stopping only when you collapsed from exhaustion.

Shame I landed on the sack of pointy moon-weapons.

Yes, but it was inspiring how you still found the strength to cringe and shriek.

basicinstructions.net

I didn't realize it at the time, but this Rocket Hat comic is unique in that it's the only time that Rocket Hat has remained motionless off-camera as well as on.

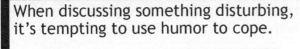

When discussing something disturbing, it's tempting to use humor to cope.

The founder of Facebook says that from now on he's killing his own meat.

Is that a euphemism?

It is now.

Some find it helpful to vividly imagine a disturbing scenario. Others do not.

So far he's killed a lobster, a pig, and a goat. He says it's to respect the animal, so I can only assume he's killing them in a fair fight.

I picture him strangling a goat, a tear rolling down his cheek as he mutters, "You fought well, brother."

That's creepy.

Did I mention he's naked?

You didn't have to.

Ground the topic in realistic, mundane details. It may seem less disturbing.

I'm sure it's more civilized than that. He's a billionaire. He probably has a special room with washable walls and a drain in the floor.

Just off his office.

An assistant brings in new animals between his meetings.

Making it more civilized isn't really helping.

Not at all.

If something really disturbs you, there is a reason. Finding this reason will teach you something about yourself.

The thing that really bugs me is, why's a billionaire eating a goat?!

THANK YOU!! Fish are delicious, and so easy to kill!

People do it for fun on their vacations!

I'm sure there are places where, for a price, he could fish naked if he really needs to.

basicinstructions.net

BASIC INSTRUCTIONS   How to Face a Medical Problem   by Scott MEYER

No matter how healthy you are normally, you'll sometimes have health problems.

The test is positive for strep throat.

Good ol' strep! It's scientifically provable, non-debilitating, and highly contagious so nobody ever wants you to come to work!

How many times have you had it?

Five in the last year. I'm a lucky man.

Often times, if there is a solution to your health problem, it will be unattractive.

We're gonna have to remove your tonsils. You'll be in pretty severe pain for seven to ten days after the operation.

That's not much of a sales pitch.

Normally "you'll be cured" is all the sales pitch I need.

I'm not normal.

Clearly.

Carefully examine all the pros and cons, and use logic to make your decision.

After the operation, you can have all the ice cream you want. What do you say to that?

I say it's a bad sign when your doctor's using the same tactics as a pedophile.

As in all things, face your fears and deal with adversity if you want to improve.

Sorry doc. I'm just a little freaked out.

Most of my tonsillectomy patients are.

Really?

Oh yeah! Of course, most of my tonsillectomy patients are also five years old.

basicinstructions.net

I had my tonsils out as an adult. It was not pleasant. One bright spot was that all of the informational literature was aimed at children. I saved one pamphlet about tonsil and adenoid removal that was titled "My T&A Adventure." Now that's how you write for multiple audiences.

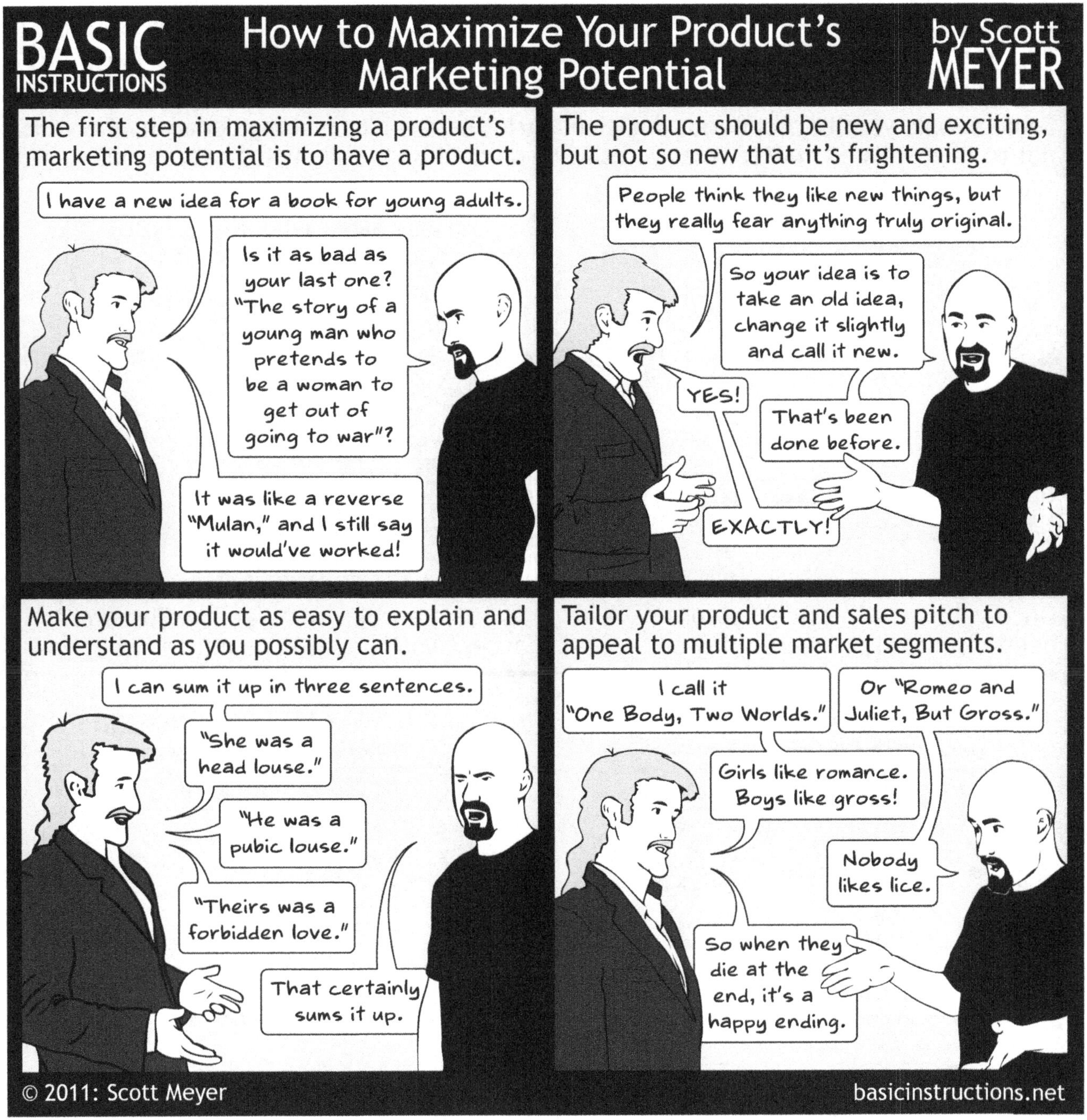

BASIC INSTRUCTIONS
How to Maximize Your Product's Marketing Potential
by Scott MEYER
The first step in maximizing a product's marketing potential is to have a product.
I have a new idea for a book for young adults.
Is it as bad as your last one? "The story of a young man who pretends to be a woman to get out of going to war"?
It was like a reverse "Mulan," and I still say it would've worked!
The product should be new and exciting, but not so new that it's frightening.
People think they like new things, but they really fear anything truly original.
So your idea is to take an old idea, change it slightly and call it new.
YES!
That's been done before.
EXACTLY!
Make your product as easy to explain and understand as you possibly can.
I can sum it up in three sentences.
"She was a head louse."
"He was a pubic louse."
"Theirs was a forbidden love."
That certainly sums it up.
Tailor your product and sales pitch to appeal to multiple market segments.
I call it "One Body, Two Worlds."
Or "Romeo and Juliet, But Gross."
Girls like romance. Boys like gross!
Nobody likes lice.
So when they die at the end, it's a happy ending.
© 2011: Scott Meyer
basicinstructions.net

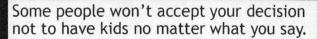

BASIC INSTRUCTIONS
How to Explain Why You've Chosen Not to Have Children
by Scott MEYER

Some people won't accept your decision not to have kids no matter what you say.

For one thing, I don't make a ton of money.

Don't let that stop you. Once you have kids you do what you have to, to make the money you need.

You've just described heroin addiction.

Not having kids is a big decision. You will no doubt have many logical reasons.

I have a family history of cancer, heart disease, spinal deformities, muscular dystrophy, and insanity.

What about your wife?

She chose to marry into my family, so that says something about her judgment.

Once your sound, logical reasons have been dismissed or ignored, lay out your emotional reasons for not reproducing.

So you're not having kids because you're afraid the child will be sick.

No. I believe evolution is trying to kill my family, and I've decided to join the winning team.

As I said earlier, some people just won't accept your decision no matter what you say, or what reasons you give.

I like kids. I just don't want one.

You'll change your mind.

You wanted kids before you had one. Have you changed your mind?

I don't have to answer that.

That's right. You don't.

basicinstructions.net

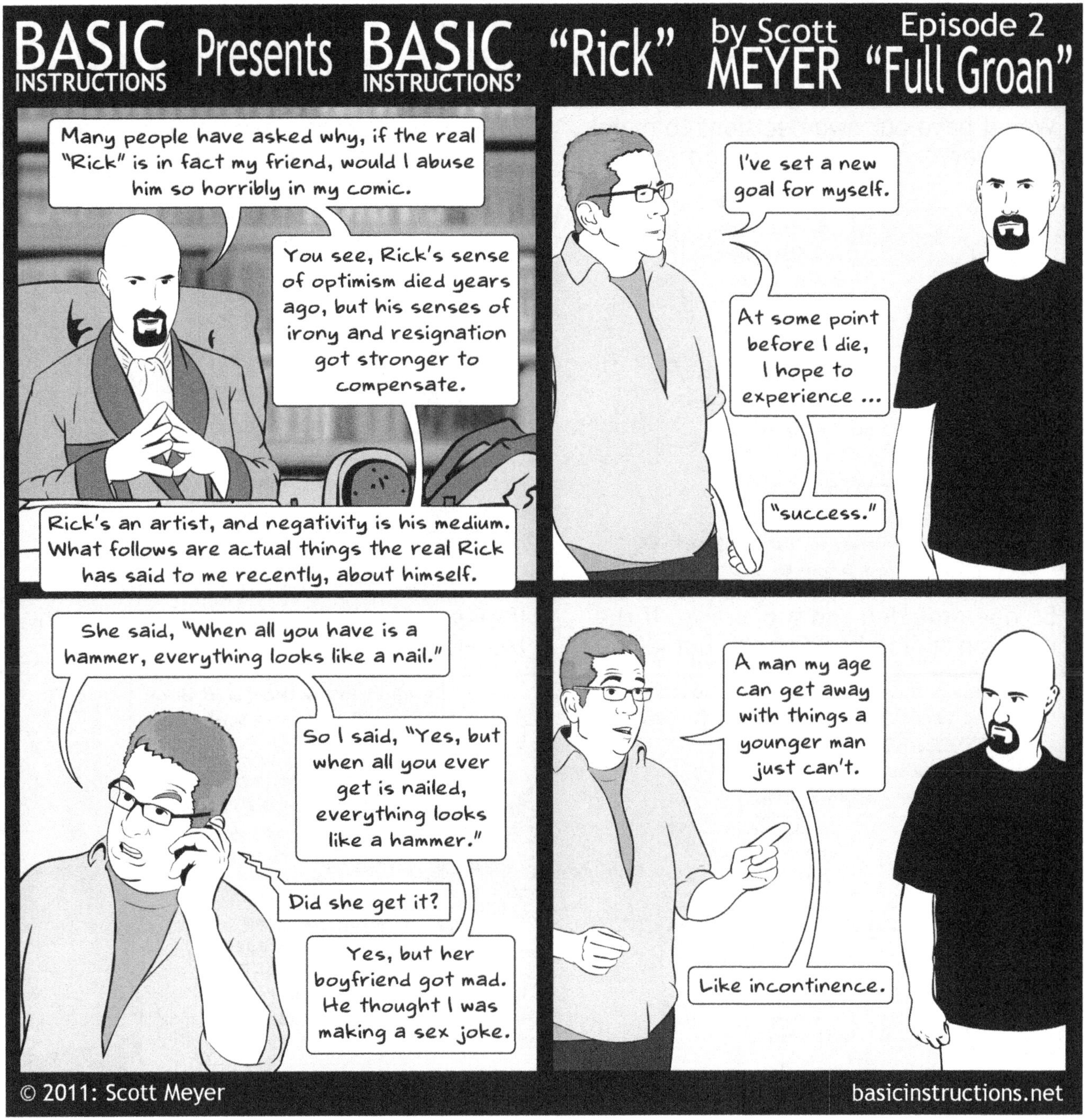
BASIC INSTRUCTIONS Presents BASIC INSTRUCTIONS' "Rick" by Scott MEYER Episode 2 "Full Groan"
Many people have asked why, if the real "Rick" is in fact my friend, would I abuse him so horribly in my comic.
You see, Rick's sense of optimism died years ago, but his senses of irony and resignation got stronger to compensate.
Rick's an artist, and negativity is his medium. What follows are actual things the real Rick has said to me recently, about himself.
I've set a new goal for myself.
At some point before I die, I hope to experience ...
"success."
She said, "When all you have is a hammer, everything looks like a nail."
So I said, "Yes, but when all you ever get is nailed, everything looks like a hammer."
Did she get it?
Yes, but her boyfriend got mad. He thought I was making a sex joke.
A man my age can get away with things a younger man just can't.
Like incontinence.
© 2011: Scott Meyer
basicinstructions.net

We all have our own decisions to make, and everyone's answers are different.

I need some advice from someone who's wiser than me.

We all do sometimes.

So I'm gonna go to a tarot card reader.

Of course, we don't all set as low a bar as you do.

People sometimes make decisions you wouldn't. They all have their reasons.

I don't put much stock in psychics, but I figure you don't really know until you try.

That depends on what you're trying.

Be open-minded and supportive. If the decision should backfire, do not gloat.

How'd it go with the tarot cards?

She pulled the death card.

I hear that doesn't really mean death.

Then she drew the ten of swords.

There're many ways

Then the "unmarked shallow grave" card.

Yeah, that seems pretty clear.

If everybody did exactly what you would, the world would be a boring place.

I didn't know the tarot deck had a "shallow grave" card.

Neither did the card reader. I'm not going back to her again.

You want a more knowledgable reader.

And who won't spit and yell, "Begone, doomed wretch."

basicinstructions.net

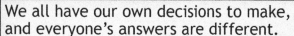

It seems like every time I've witnessed a tarot reading, the Death card has been pulled and the reader has blurted out, "It doesn't mean death." This is just an idea, but maybe they could CHANGE THE NAME OF THE CARD! I suggest calling it "the False Alarm."

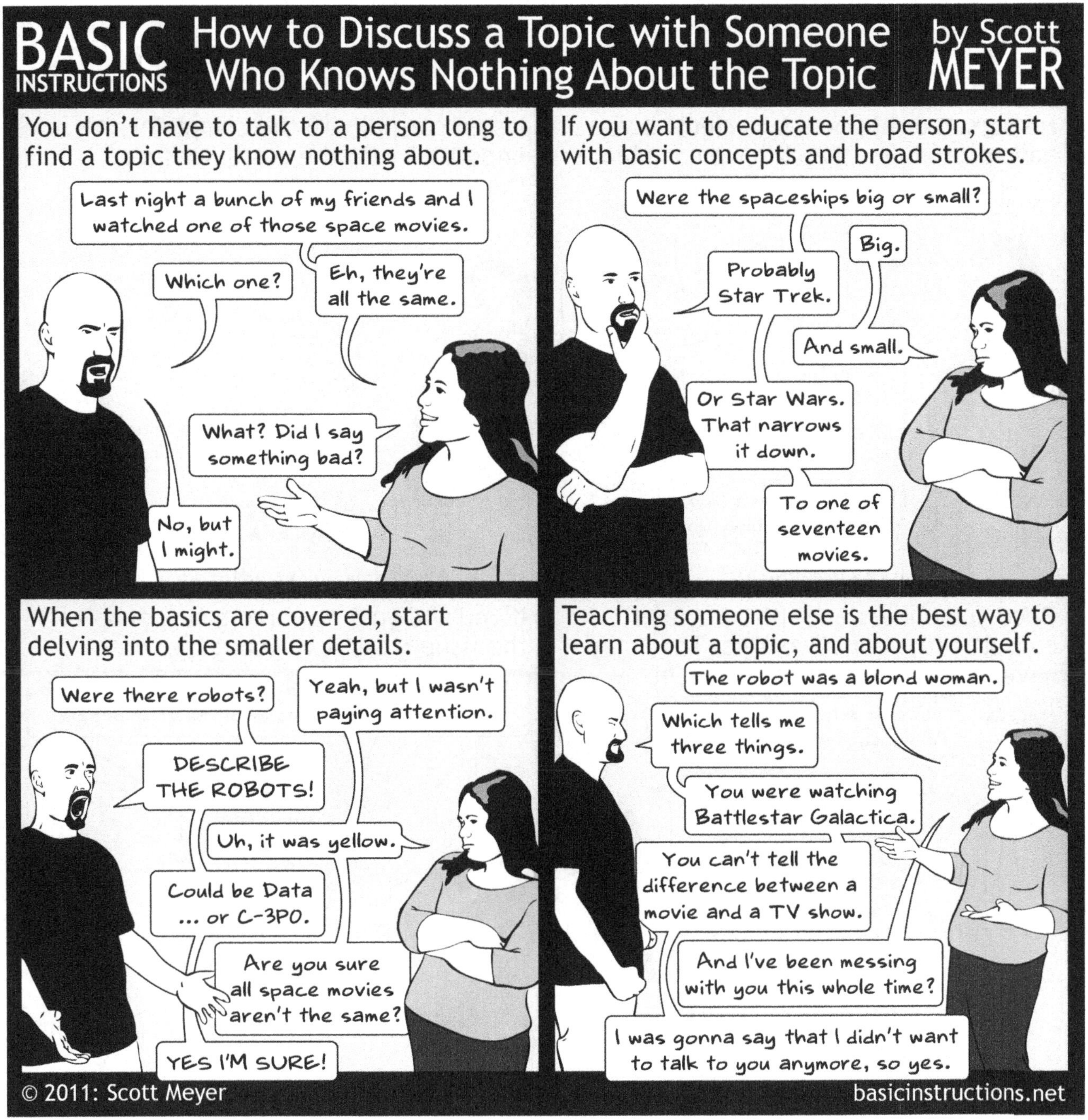
BASIC INSTRUCTIONS
How to Discuss a Topic with Someone Who Knows Nothing About the Topic
by Scott MEYER
You don't have to talk to a person long to find a topic they know nothing about.
Last night a bunch of my friends and I watched one of those space movies.
Which one?
Eh, they're all the same.
What? Did I say something bad?
No, but I might.
If you want to educate the person, start with basic concepts and broad strokes.
Were the spaceships big or small?
Big.
And small.
Probably Star Trek.
Or Star Wars. That narrows it down.
To one of seventeen movies.
When the basics are covered, start delving into the smaller details.
Were there robots?
Yeah, but I wasn't paying attention.
DESCRIBE THE ROBOTS!
Uh, it was yellow.
Could be Data ... or C-3PO.
Are you sure all space movies aren't the same?
YES I'M SURE!
Teaching someone else is the best way to learn about a topic, and about yourself.
The robot was a blond woman.
Which tells me three things.
You were watching Battlestar Galactica.
You can't tell the difference between a movie and a TV show.
And I've been messing with you this whole time?
I was gonna say that I didn't want to talk to you anymore, so yes.
© 2011: Scott Meyer
basicinstructions.net

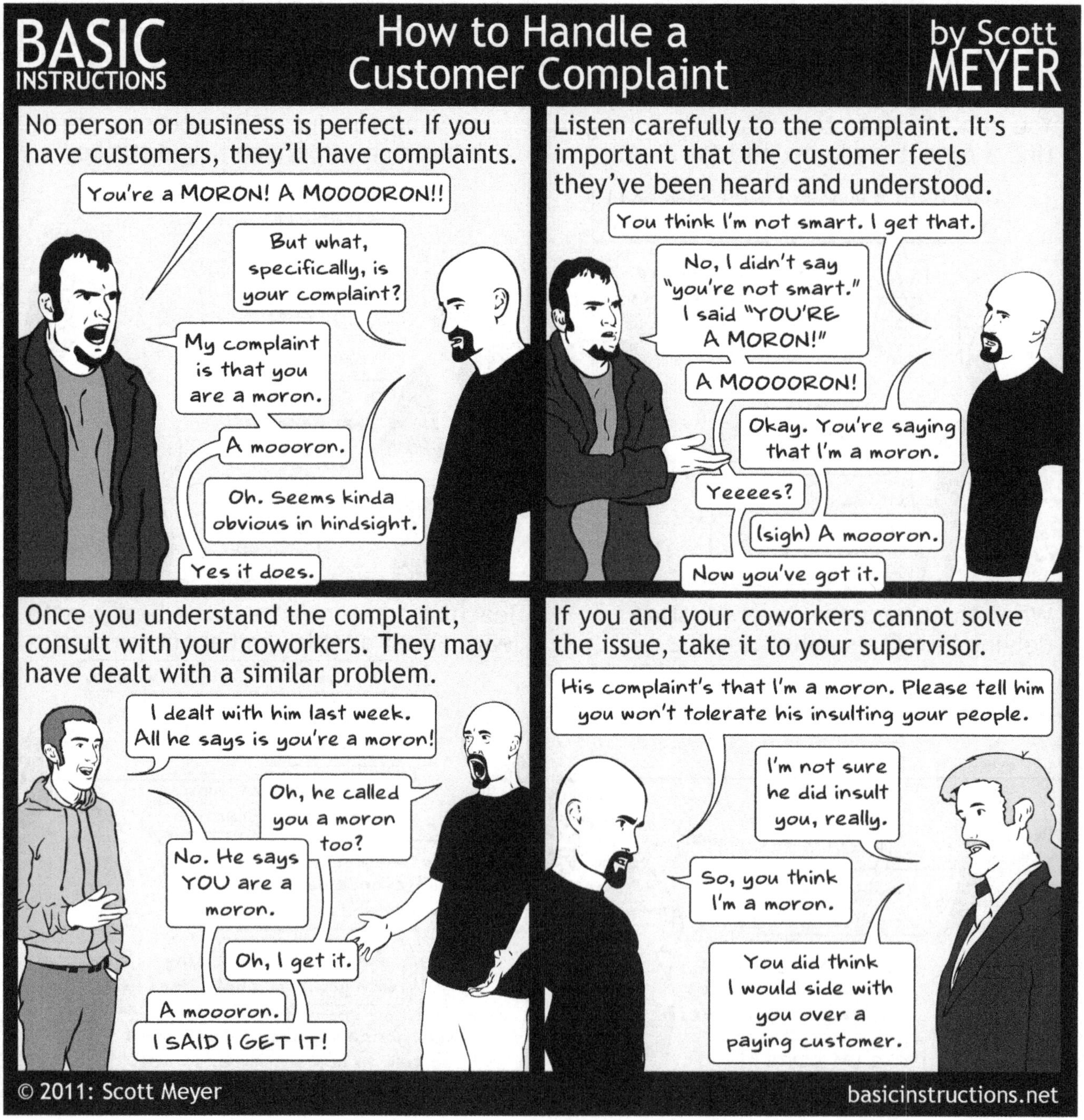
BASIC INSTRUCTIONS
How to Handle a Customer Complaint
by Scott MEYER
No person or business is perfect. If you have customers, they'll have complaints.
You're a MORON! A MOOOORON!!
But what, specifically, is your complaint?
My complaint is that you are a moron.
A moooron.
Oh. Seems kinda obvious in hindsight.
Yes it does.
Listen carefully to the complaint. It's important that the customer feels they've been heard and understood.
You think I'm not smart. I get that.
No, I didn't say "you're not smart." I said "YOU'RE A MORON!"
A MOOOORON!
Okay. You're saying that I'm a moron.
Yeeees?
(sigh) A moooron.
Now you've got it.
Once you understand the complaint, consult with your coworkers. They may have dealt with a similar problem.
I dealt with him last week. All he says is you're a moron!
Oh, he called you a moron too?
No. He says YOU are a moron.
Oh, I get it.
A moooron.
I SAID I GET IT!
If you and your coworkers cannot solve the issue, take it to your supervisor.
His complaint's that I'm a moron. Please tell him you won't tolerate his insulting your people.
I'm not sure he did insult you, really.
So, you think I'm a moron.
You did think I would side with you over a paying customer.
© 2011: Scott Meyer
basicinstructions.net

No two people are the same. Because of this, your actions may cause confusion.

What is this?!

The RJ-17 form I filled out yesterday.

It makes no sense.

To you. You've never understood my methods.

That is true.

Explain your actions and the thinking behind them at the most basic level.

You wrote the same thing in every blank.

I strive for simplicity.

It's not even a real word. "BGDAAAAA."

It's one syllable. You say the first three letters all at once.

BGDAAAA!

Again, simplicity.

Simple is one word for it.

Once the basics are covered, get into the specific details of what you did, and why.

I say it when I'm frustrated. Or shocked. Or scared. Or hurt. Or if I drop something. And sometimes when I wake up in the morning.

I think I've heard you use it as a greeting.

When greeting you, yes, I have.

Explaining yourself helps others learn about you, and helps you learn how to better communicate with others.

By responding to the questions with a raw emotional reaction, I've told you more about myself than mere facts ever could.

I'm your employer. I don't care about your emotions.

Bgdaaa.

basicinstructions.net

This comic was written to explain how to pronounce my favorite exclamation of shock and anger, "Bgdaaaaa." To be honest, the first three letters come out unidentifiable as they try to force their way out of my larynx at the same time like the Three Stooges.

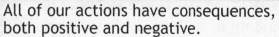

BASIC INSTRUCTIONS
How to Face the Consequences
by Scott MEYER

All of our actions have consequences, both positive and negative.

I like to think of this office as a family. I'm like the father of that family.

Unfortunately, there comes a time in every father's life when he has to fire one of his kids.

Consider what you did that caused the consequences to determine if they are fair, or to formulate a defense.

I told you to stop putting punctuation in your RJ-17 form.

But it makes the form more informative by adding emotional content.

The company doesn't care about your emotions.

It's just one more way that we're like a family.

If you are in the wrong, face it like an adult. If not, defend yourself to the end.

But it makes the form so much more evocative.

Name: Scott, exclamation mark!

Occupation: Office manager, question mark.

Termination date: soon.

Question mark?

Period.

You can't prevent consequences, but you can at least make your position clear.

I did make a change. This time I put the same punctuation on every answer.

It was a question mark and an exclamation mark.

It's called an "interrobang."

"Interrobang," is that even a real thing?!

You just used one.

Really?!

Now you're just messing with me, aren't you.

basicinstructions.net

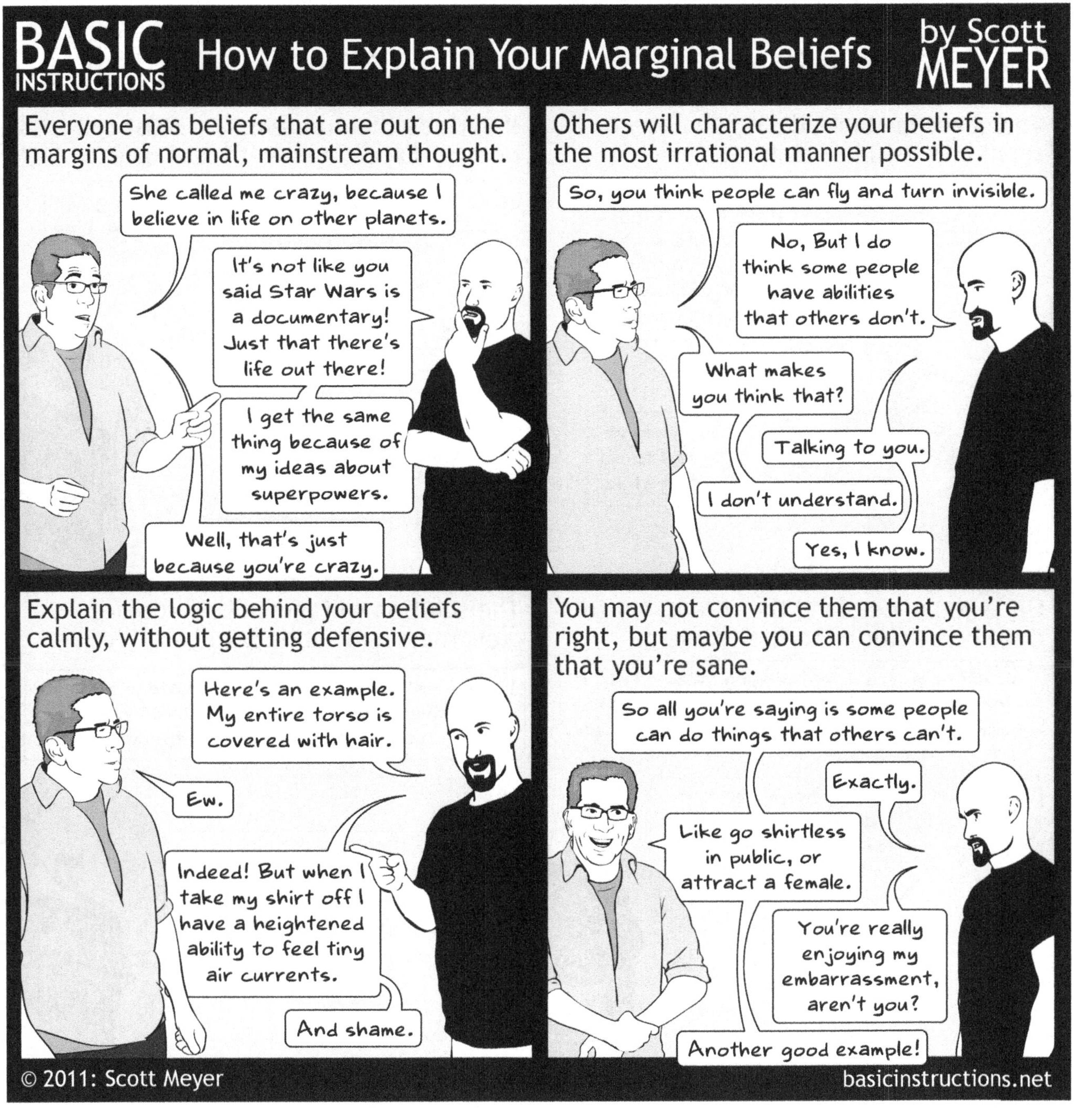

BASIC INSTRUCTIONS
How to Explain Your Marginal Beliefs
by Scott MEYER
Everyone has beliefs that are out on the margins of normal, mainstream thought.
She called me crazy, because I believe in life on other planets.
It's not like you said Star Wars is a documentary! Just that there's life out there!
I get the same thing because of my ideas about superpowers.
Well, that's just because you're crazy.
Others will characterize your beliefs in the most irrational manner possible.
So, you think people can fly and turn invisible.
No, But I do think some people have abilities that others don't.
What makes you think that?
Talking to you.
I don't understand.
Yes, I know.
Explain the logic behind your beliefs calmly, without getting defensive.
Here's an example. My entire torso is covered with hair.
Ew.
Indeed! But when I take my shirt off I have a heightened ability to feel tiny air currents.
And shame.
You may not convince them that you're right, but maybe you can convince them that you're sane.
So all you're saying is some people can do things that others can't.
Exactly.
Like go shirtless in public, or attract a female.
You're really enjoying my embarrassment, aren't you?
Another good example!
© 2011: Scott Meyer
basicinstructions.net

The seeds of Mankind's ruin will seem small and harmless at first.

The guards in this game just dodge your clumsy blows until you eventually fall off of something tall and die.

Yes. They've adapted to my fighting style.

If you see the problem, you must tell people. Expect to meet resistance.

And that's when I realized, by using adaptive A.I. in video games, we're teaching the machines how best to kill us.

By dodging and waiting for you to accidentally kill yourself?

In my case. In yours, they'll probably dodge and wait for me to take you with me.

Once you understand the threat, try to develop a solution to the problem.

If you're worried that playing video games is teaching computers how to kill us and take over, you can play online against real people.

Then I'd be teaching foul-mouthed twelve-year-olds how to kill us and take over.

Machines would be preferable.

The solution will most likely require cleverness and subtlety to be effective.

I plan to shape the machines' strategy by being selective about what games I play. From now on, it's nothing but casual smartphone games.

With any luck, when the machines make their move, their fortress will be made of plywood, glass blocks, and live pigs.

Looking at this comic again, it strikes me that I paint a nightmare scenario in which the machines take over, but that our current actual plan is for the foul-mouthed twelve-year-olds to do it. All kidding aside, I might have to start rooting for the machines.

BASIC INSTRUCTIONS

How to Evaluate Other People's Deep Philosophical Insights

by Scott MEYER

Anytime anyone has a deep philosophical insight, they will feel a need to share it.

Show them the courtesy of listening to their thoughts with an open mind.

If you don't understand what they mean at first, let them expound at length.

Once you understand the idea, consider the person who thought of it to help decide if the concept has any merit.

basicinstructions.net

How to Recuperate from a Minor Surgical Procedure

Listen closely to your doctor's warnings. They are just trying to prepare you for what they know is coming.

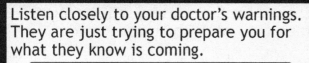

On the third day after the tonsillectomy, you'll be ready to start moaning.

It'll really be bad enough that I'll want to moan three days later?

You'll want to moan immediately, but we don't want you to strain yourself.

Do your best to follow your doctor's advice, and to keep a positive attitude.

Uhhhhhhhhhhhhhhhhhhhhhhhh.

He said you could moan, not that you have to.

Fine. I'll describe my situation more articulately.

The inside of my mouth tastes like scabs.

Please start moaning again.

Try to distract yourself from the discomfort by keeping yourself busy.

I'm seeing how long I can go without swallowing. I'm up to three hours.

I couldn't do that.

The key is to convince yourself that it's okay to drool.

I couldn't do that either.

You'll want to resume normal activities as soon as possible, but it is a mistake to push yourself too hard too soon.

How are you today?

Mostly back to normal. Dr Pepper doesn't taste quite right though.

Then you're back to normal. Dr Pepper never tastes quite right. It's practically their slogan.

basicinstructions.net

BASIC INSTRUCTIONS

How to Deal with a Disinterested Audience

by Scott MEYER

Panel 1

Anytime you talk to people there will be a chance that they won't care about the topic being discussed as much as you do.

Wanna see something?

No.

Are you sure? It's pretty cool.

Maybe, but it's much cooler to act unimpressed by everything.

Panel 2

If they truly don't care, don't continue. If they care a little, use your judgment as to whether to continue or not.

So what were you going to show us?

You want me to show you what you don't want me to show you.

Look, do you want to show us or not?

I'm really not sure anymore.

Panel 3

If you do decide to continue, do so with all the enthusiasm you can muster.

Well here it is! It's the world's oldest tarp!

And the world's largest anticlimax!

Panel 4

If the topic is interesting, your audience may be interested in spite of themselves.

So that's the world's oldest tarp, huh?

Yup, right here ...

Under this ordinary tarp.

Of course. You wouldn't want the world's oldest tarp to get damaged.

basicinstructions.net

Somewhere out there, someone does own the world's oldest tarp. My hope is that it sits on the world's least interesting pedestal, in the world's most poorly attended museum. I'd bet it's somewhere in Kissimmee, FL.

BASIC INSTRUCTIONS

How to Discuss the Differences Between Men and Women

by Scott MEYER

Start slowly and carefully, like you're walking on thin ice, because you are.

Lets start with differences that are generally recognized as safe to discuss.

Fine. Men and women are different genders.

Indeed, and that concludes the differences that are generally recognized as safe to discuss.

Wait for someone to say something that exposes themselves as a bigot so you can exclude them from the conversation.

Men and women approach marriage like they approach major purchases.

Women buy houses and fix them up. Men buy sports cars and watch them depreciate.

Your wife left you.

She said I was going to take too much work.

One way to be fair is to focus on your own gender's perceived weaknesses.

Men are easier to kill. Take the movie Psycho. If it was reversed, and a man in a shower was interrupted by a woman, he wouldn't scream.

He'd invite her to join him.

He might scream, THEN invite her.

Eh, it'd be more of a whoop.

The conversation is difficult, but it's also the best way to learn about each other.

But if the roles from Psycho were reversed, the woman'd be dressed as an old man and holding a knife.

I know. His last words would be "Oh, so that's what you're into. That's cool."

basicinstructions.net

Of course, all of the statements in this strip are gross overgeneralizations. I would say that all gross overgeneralizations are inaccurate, but to do so would create a logic paradox that might destroy my computer, if Star Trek can be believed.

BASIC INSTRUCTIONS
How to Handle a Continuity Error
by Scott MEYER

A continuity error is when the internal logic of a story does not hold up.

> Omnipresent Man, Mr. Everywhere, if you're both everywhere at the same time, how could you have only met recently?

> Many people have asked us that.

> You've never answered.

> Many people can't take a hint.

Sometimes, if you're lucky, it's due to a misconception on the reader's part.

> We weren't always omnipresent.

> We're everywhere, not everywhen!

> Someone who's present at every point in history would be really hard to write.

> YES! LET ME BE CLEAR! NO SUCH SUPERHERO EXISTS, OR EVER WILL!

One common way to deal with continuity errors is to give a character memory loss.

> Wouldn't you have been there for his birth?

> I only got my powers a few years ago, and I block out memories of witnessing childbirths anyway.

> Why?

> Because I witness them from inside the birth canal. Would you wanna remember that?

The best solution is to come up with a logical explanation that fixes the issue.

> Look, we're everywhere, but we can't pay attention to everything.

> For a while we didn't notice each other.

> Then for a while we acted like we didn't notice each other.

> That didn't last long. It's hard to avoid eye contact when you're both everywhere.

© 2011: Scott Meyer

basicinstructions.net

BASIC INSTRUCTIONS

How to Participate in "Group Learning"

by Scott MEYER

You thought you were done with it when you left school, but group learning still comes up sometimes in the "real world."

Attention employees: It's time for group learning.

Today's lesson is called "Your Job: That thing none of you are doing."

I'll start by asking you a question.

Why are you all so useless?

The majority of the energy expended is spent avoiding answering any questions.

Who wants to answer the question?

Fine, who's brave enough to answer the question?

So none of you will answer a question.

Seems to me we just answered two.

Answering questions is a fine opportunity to make yourself look good, or to steer the conversation where you want it.

Sir, I think the real problem is that nobody else here's as good an employee as I am.

I agree ...

... that if he were your best employee, that would be a real problem.

If the group is stuck on a specific issue, reframing the problem can help everyone see it differently, and might help.

Is the problem that we aren't trying to do the job, or that we are trying, but doing the job badly?

Both. Lots of both.

What if we promise to narrow it down to one?

I start crying.

DONE!

basicinstructions.net

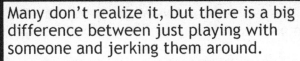

Many don't realize it, but there is a big difference between just playing with someone and jerking them around.

I want you to come in to work on Saturday.

I don't want to.

I'll be here too.

That doesn't make it better.

But the fact that you don't want to makes it better for me.

Ideally, playing will be fun for both parties, whereas "jerking around" is twice as fun, but only for one party.

If I do come in on my day off ...

And you will.

What will I be doing?

I'll come up with something fun.

For me.

To watch you do.

There has to be some form of fairness in the game for it to ever be enjoyable.

You're kidding.

Dead serious!

No, really?

Yes, really!

I don't believe it.

You'd better!

Ugh, fine! I'll come in on my day off.

HA! You're so gullible! I was just kidding!

%#@%!!

But since you offered, do come in.

Of course, if you find yourself being "jerked around," you can often make it more fair by "changing the game."

Where are you?!

At home.

You said you'd be at the office on our day off too!

Yeah, I was still kidding when I said that. So, are you at the office?

As far as you know. I could leave you some evidence, if you like.

I'll take your word for it.

Wise.

basicinstructions.net

BASIC INSTRUCTIONS

How to Embrace Change

by Scott MEYER

Surprising and unsettling as it can be, the truth is that change is inevitable.

I went into a toy store today.

How was it?

Strange.

When I was a kid, I wanted all the toys, and my mom wouldn't pay for any of 'em.

Now, I still want all the toys, but I won't pay for any of 'em.

Change often follows a set, predictable course, which is not all that comforting.

The toys are all ten times awesomer now!

How much better can they be?

Nerf is now primarily a weapons manufacturer.

I see your point.

People fear large disruptions, but most change is small and incremental.

Nerf makes everything from battle axes to sniper rifles.

Back when they still just made sporting goods, what did you and your brothers do with your Nerf footballs?

Throw them at each other's heads.

Though change is unavoidable, there are certain things that will remain constant.

We had to use our imaginations and our throwing arms to pretend to murder each other. Like my father before me, I declare kids today have it too easy!

You sound jealous.

LIKE MY FATHER BEFORE ME!

basicinstructions.net

All I'm saying is that it's plausible for a kid to walk into a toy store with $200 and walk out with a full ninja costume, an automatic Nerf gun, and a set of working night-vision goggles. When I was a kid, every part of that would have amazed me, including the idea of a kid having $200.

How to Make a "Clip Show"

by Scott MEYER

A "Clip Show" is when a long-running TV show makes a "new" episode constructed mostly of clips from previous episodes.

I've got no ideas.

What do the writers for The Simpsons do when they're out of ideas?

Keep going for five more seasons.

The key to an entertaining clip show is finding a plausible reason for characters to be remembering past events.

You insult me a lot.

Yes. What are some of your favorite insults I have hurled at you?

I DON'T HAVE ANY FAVORITES!!

That's fine. I've got plenty.

It's important to pick your clips carefully. Also, frame them in a way that enhances them. Don't just let them lie there.

If it's worth doing, it's worth doing right.

Or in your case, having someone else do it.

That's not true!

I've spoken to ex-girlfriends of yours who would disagree.

That one made me cry.

I remember. You even cried badly.

An occasional clip show can be fun, but you owe it to your viewers to get back to normal production as soon as possible.

30 minutes and 58 insulting clips later:

Yessir, we've had a lot of fun insulting you, and I'm sure we both look forward to continuing for years to come.

I dread each new day.

SEE! You don't even look forward to stuff right!

basicinstructions.net

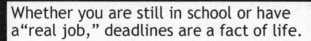

BASIC INSTRUCTIONS
How to Handle a Deadline
by Scott MEYER

Whether you are still in school or have a "real job," deadlines are a fact of life.

I'm delivering a speech and a slide presentation in three days.

You'll write it, and assemble the presentation.

What are you going to do?

Wait for you to finish.

The subject is teamwork. So get to work, team.

One strategy is to break a large job up into smaller incremental jobs, each with its own mandatory completion date.

I've divided the job I have to finish in three days into six tasks that each have to be done in half a day.

So you've divided the pressure by six.

No, I've multiplied it by six.

I figure the sooner I burn out, the sooner I'm done.

Your own mental attitude is the key. Try to view the deadline as a challenge.

It's like a video game. I finish the "make an outline" level, then defeat the "write the speech" boss-battle.

Before I do the "construct the presentation" level, I hunt for "collectables" like images and statistics.

And the boss's gratitude is like an "achievement point" ... utterly worthless.

Deadlines are stressful, but there's great satisfaction in knowing that you did your job well, and finished on time.

The presentation's done.

The meeting's been postponed.

You'll have to redo the presentation so it's up to date.

When's the meeting?

I'll tell you three days before. You've proved that's enough time. Good work!

That sounded sarcastic.

REALLY?!

basicinstructions.net

The idea of treating a real world task like a videogame is something I actually do. Making Basic Instructions is like a videogame, in that I monkey around with my computer doing things I enjoy. The only difference is that I have a finished comic when I complete a level.

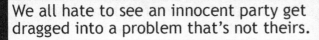

Panel 1: We all hate to see an innocent party get dragged into a problem that's not theirs.

Now that we've captured this handsome member of the League of Heroes, Rocket Hat will rush to his aid, and into our trap.

You haven't studied our organization very closely, have you?

Panel 2: Of course, we hate it worse when they try to drag you into it with them.

Omnipresent Man, are you here?

The answer to that question is always the same. "Yes."

Will you help me?

The answer to that question is always the same.

"I don't want to get involved."

Yes.

Panel 3: A desperate person will grab at anything or anyone that might be able to help.

Judger! You see all!

Yes.

Can you help me?

No, but I can judge your reactions.

That's real helpful.

Sarcasm noted.

Panel 4: If it's none of your business, stay out of it. The situation will resolve itself.

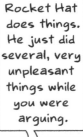

What's the point in being in a team of Superheroes if I'm the only one who does anything?

Rocket Hat does things. He just did several, very unpleasant things while you were arguing.

You're free to go.

basicinstructions.net

127

BASIC INSTRUCTIONS

How to Help Someone See Their Mistake

by Scott MEYER

Often, people will know they have made a mistake, but will not know what it was.

Our boss hates me for no reason!

He has a reason.

You gonna tell me what it is?

No, it's more fun if you try to guess.

Describe their actions for them. They might spot their mistake on their own.

The first day you worked here, you spent the whole day telling him how much better they did things at your old office.

They did lots of things right there.

They fired you.

I'm not talking about that.

Are you sure?

If they still don't see their mistake, point it out as diplomatically as you can.

He was showing me how to do everything the wrong way.

No, he was showing the right way, in his opinion.

He likes things done a certain way.

Badly?!

And inefficiently, so we make fewer errors than we might otherwise.

Sadly, you can't make someone get it. They'll either see the problem or not.

You can make suggestions, but in the end, the right way is the way the person paying you wants it done.

But if it's wrong?

Then that's his mistake.

But I'm the one making it.

Welcome to life at the mistake factory.

basicinstructions.net

If your supervisor insists that you do something wrong, there's no upside to doing it the right way against their wishes. The best case scenario is that they'll never notice. More likely, they'll find out and punish you. The worst case is that they'll get credit for your intelligence.

We all have flaws. Some of our flaws are obvious to us. Others must be pointed out by someone close to us.

You're easily startled.

BGDAAAAAAH!

Also, we all have problems that may or may not be caused by our own flaws.

WHAT?! WHAT?! WHAT IS IT?!

I just called to see how you are.

I'M FINE!

Really? You sound freaked out.

That's 'cause I'm so super-fine that it freaks me right out!

Now I'm a little freaked out.

Often our shortcomings are connected to our problems in a way that's hard to see, but seems obvious in hindsight.

BWOOOOM ... BWOOOOM ... BWOOOOM

BDGAAAH! MY PHONE!

You know you're jumpy, so you chose the red alert siren from Star Trek for your ringtone.

BDGAAAH! MY POOR DECISION MAKING SKILLS!

Take action to fix the problem. Just know you can't eliminate all problems, but you can trade them for better ones.

How's that Hawaiian music ringtone I got you?

That's good!

It makes me drowsy.

Earlier I dozed off, and it startled me.

That's impressive, in a weird kinda way.

Which is usually the way I'm impressive.

basicinstructions.net

BASIC INSTRUCTIONS

How to Explain Your Tastes

by Scott MEYER

Not everyone will share your tastes. You may feel the urge to explain yourself.

Why are you drinking Dr Pepper?

Because I like it. Is that so hard to understand?

NO, I understand. Either your taste buds are broken or you don't know what "like" means.

Try to help others see the things you like through your eyes. This is the method wine connoisseurs use ... to bore people.

Dr Pepper is different from other soft drinks.

Other soft drinks taste good.

Dr Pepper has a subtle, complex flavor profile.

There's caramel, vanilla ...

Prune.

Perhaps, but it never overpowers the caramel.

Often people's distaste may be based on misconceptions that you can clear up.

Dr Pepper has NEVER contained prunes.

If it did, it would say "made with real fruit" on the label.

Fine, It's not made with prunes.

Thank you!

It's made with "chemical prune substitute."

If all else fails, it might help if you can get them to sample the thing you like.

Try it.

No!

No!

Come on.

Scared?

LOOK, IF YOU'RE GONNA INSIST THAT I TRY DR PEPPER, I'M NOT GOING TO DISCUSS IT WITH YOU ANYMORE!!

I'll just have to live with that.

basicinstructions.net

They always bring up prune juice, like it's poison. Seriously, pick any carbonated beverage, read the ingredients, then imagine someone gave you the choice to drink all of that, or a shot glass of prune juice. I'm not saying you'd pick prune juice, but you'd have to think about it.

How to Have Nice Things

When you have something nice, the whole world seems bent on destroying it.

The cat barfed on the cream-colored carpet again.

It's a shame we can't train him to barf on the tile.

If I could train cats to barf on a specific target, I'd have lots more cats and much unhappier enemies.

The key to keeping something nice can be simply repairing it as it gets damaged.

I got a pet stain remover. From now on, when the cat barfs, all I have to do is perform a simple five-step procedure.

And it completely erases the stain?

No. Accepting that is step one.

Keeping your things in good condition Isn't complicated. It just takes effort.

So you're hauling out a heavy loud machine every time the cat barfs to not quite prevent damage to a carpet that's already ruined.

I don't see the point.

I might be doing something pointless, but at least I'm doing something.

Some items tend to look better with use and wear, if only to their owner.

How's that cat stain shampooer?

It's in pristine condition. I only used it twice.

So did your cat stop throwing up?

No, I just decided to stop fighting it. In two more months I can pass the carpet off as being a giraffe print.

basicinstructions.net

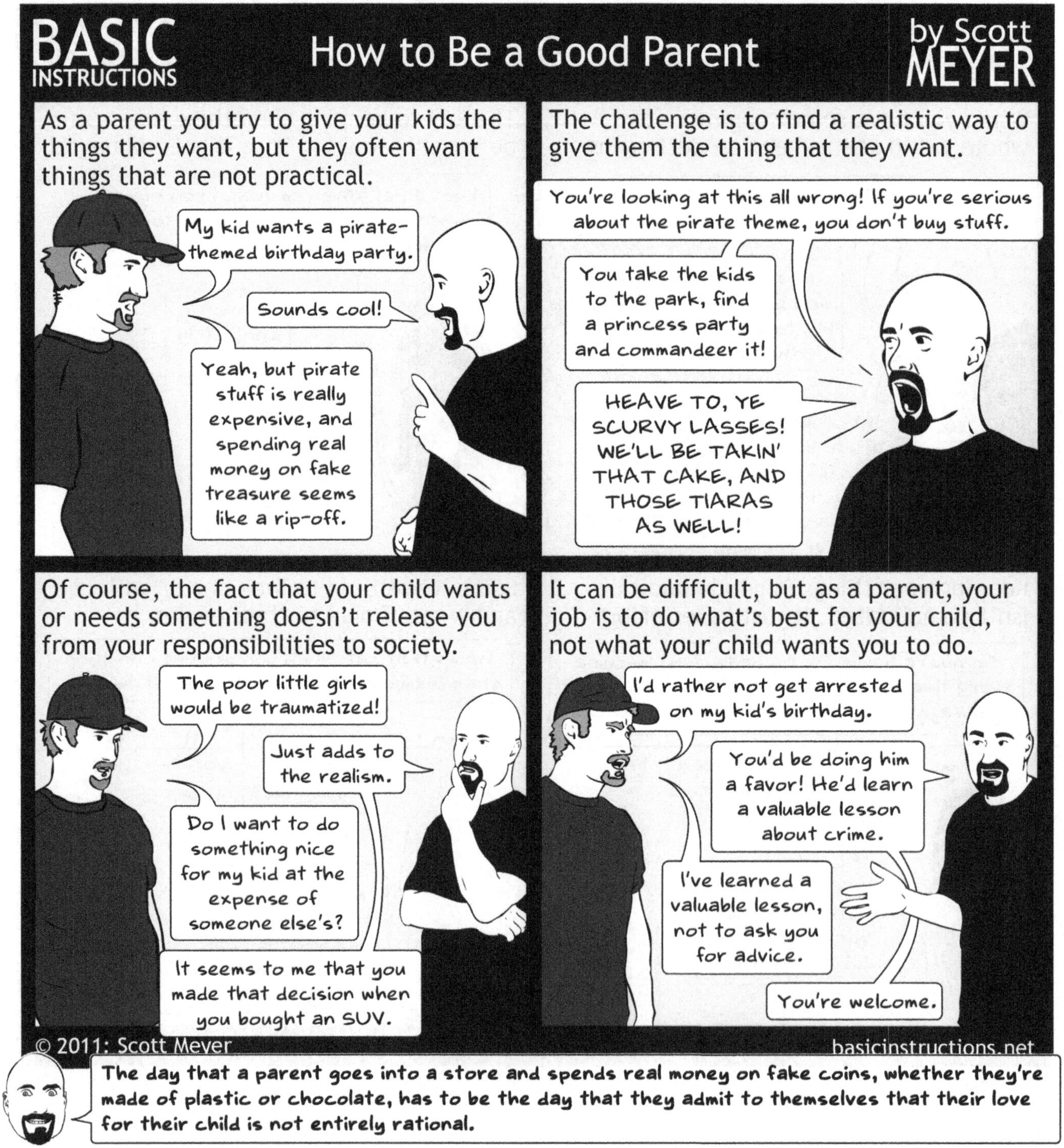
BASIC INSTRUCTIONS
How to Be a Good Parent
by Scott MEYER
As a parent you try to give your kids the things they want, but they often want things that are not practical.
My kid wants a pirate-themed birthday party.
Sounds cool!
Yeah, but pirate stuff is really expensive, and spending real money on fake treasure seems like a rip-off.
The challenge is to find a realistic way to give them the thing that they want.
You're looking at this all wrong! If you're serious about the pirate theme, you don't buy stuff.
You take the kids to the park, find a princess party and commandeer it!
HEAVE TO, YE SCURVY LASSES! WE'LL BE TAKIN' THAT CAKE, AND THOSE TIARAS AS WELL!
Of course, the fact that your child wants or needs something doesn't release you from your responsibilities to society.
The poor little girls would be traumatized!
Just adds to the realism.
Do I want to do something nice for my kid at the expense of someone else's?
It seems to me that you made that decision when you bought an SUV.
It can be difficult, but as a parent, your job is to do what's best for your child, not what your child wants you to do.
I'd rather not get arrested on my kid's birthday.
You'd be doing him a favor! He'd learn a valuable lesson about crime.
I've learned a valuable lesson, not to ask you for advice.
You're welcome.
© 2011: Scott Meyer
basicinstructions.net
The day that a parent goes into a store and spends real money on fake coins, whether they're made of plastic or chocolate, has to be the day that they admit to themselves that their love for their child is not entirely rational.

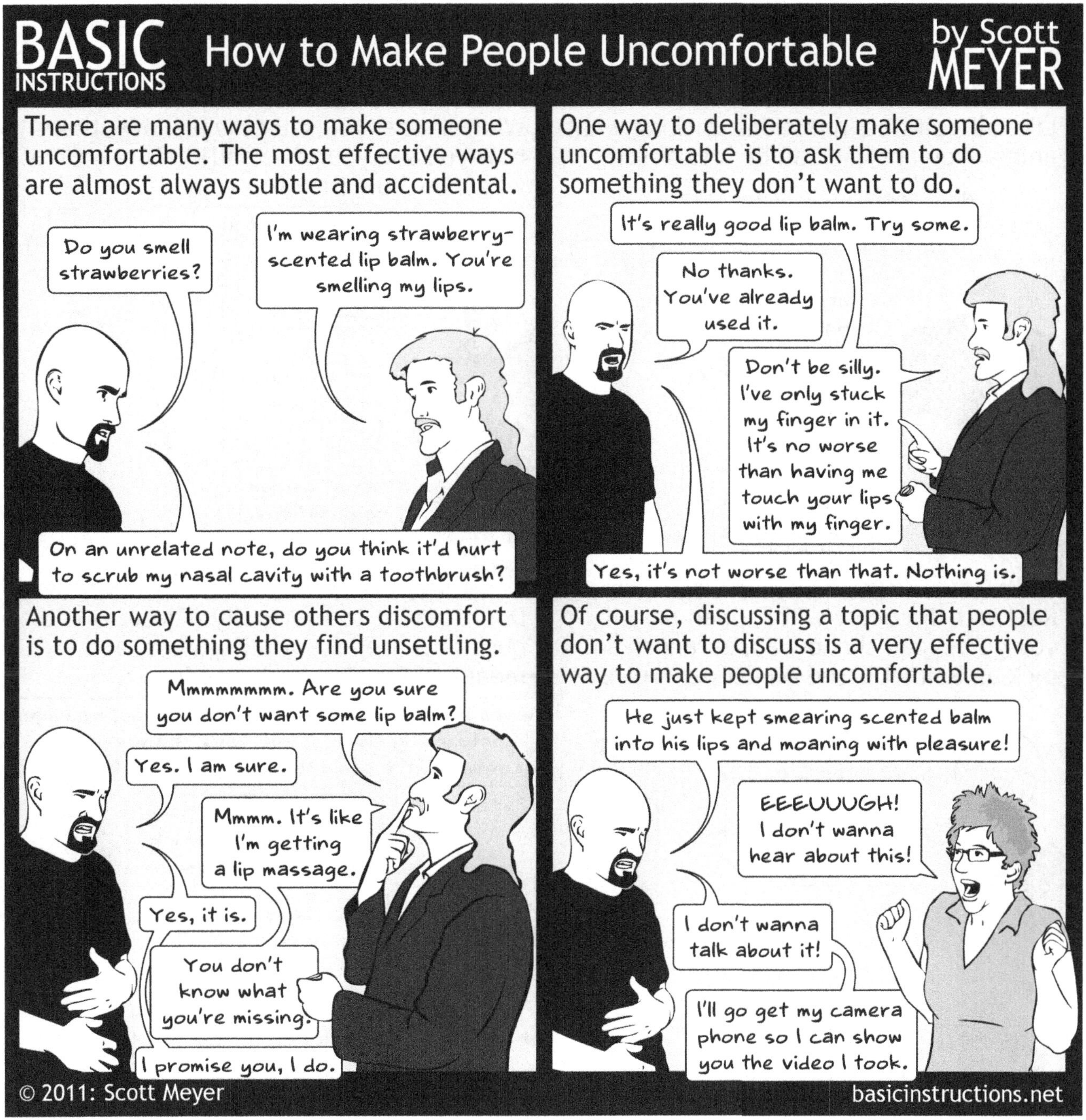
BASIC INSTRUCTIONS
How to Make People Uncomfortable
by Scott MEYER
There are many ways to make someone uncomfortable. The most effective ways are almost always subtle and accidental.
Do you smell strawberries?
I'm wearing strawberry-scented lip balm. You're smelling my lips.
On an unrelated note, do you think it'd hurt to scrub my nasal cavity with a toothbrush?
One way to deliberately make someone uncomfortable is to ask them to do something they don't want to do.
It's really good lip balm. Try some.
No thanks. You've already used it.
Don't be silly. I've only stuck my finger in it. It's no worse than having me touch your lips with my finger.
Yes, it's not worse than that. Nothing is.
Another way to cause others discomfort is to do something they find unsettling.
Mmmmmmmm. Are you sure you don't want some lip balm?
Yes. I am sure.
Mmmm. It's like I'm getting a lip massage.
Yes, it is.
You don't know what you're missing.
I promise you, I do.
Of course, discussing a topic that people don't want to discuss is a very effective way to make people uncomfortable.
He just kept smearing scented balm into his lips and moaning with pleasure!
EEEUUUGH! I don't wanna hear about this!
I don't wanna talk about it!
I'll go get my camera phone so I can show you the video I took.
© 2011: Scott Meyer
basicinstructions.net

BASIC INSTRUCTIONS

How to Pick Which Animal You're Most Like

by Scott MEYER

Like all pointless questions, picking what animal you are like can be lots of fun.

What animal you select will show others how you see yourself, and their reactions will show how they see you.

Real self-discovery will happen only if you go beyond shallow appearances and pick an animal based on deeper truths.

Don't take it too seriously. These sorts of questions are essentially games, and are meant to be silly, harmless fun.

basicinstructions.net

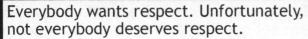

BASIC INSTRUCTIONS

How to Give Somebody the Respect They Deserve

by Scott MEYER

Everybody wants respect. Unfortunately, not everybody deserves respect.

You're a Windows guy. You must be happy Steve Jobs retired.

Not at all! I really respect Steve Jobs.

You should. He invented the smart phone.

Sadly, I don't have the same respect for his fans.

Respect has to be based on real accomplishments to mean anything.

I had a Treo, a touch screen phone that ran apps, played music and videos, and browsed the web, years before the iPhone.

And it did all those things in a way the iPhone seldom does.

Badly.

When deciding if you respect someone, look at what they've actually done.

He didn't make the first computer, just the first computer you could use.

And the first mp3 player worth buying.

And the first smart phone that worked.

And the first tablet people actually want.

He's the kid who copies off of your test, then gets a better grade than you.

Look at their accomplishments and their failings, then give credit where it's due.

I've heard that he's a dictator and a bully, but my PC and my Android phone wouldn't be nearly as good as they are if not for Steve Jobs demonstrating what's possible.

Wonder what he'll do now that he's retired.

Hopefully, the same thing as Bill Gates, but better.

© 2011: Scott Meyer

basicinstructions.net

Clearly, this comic was written before Steve Jobs passed away. Sadly, the consensus at the time was that he didn't look well, and wouldn't enjoy a long retirement. While I'm not an Apple guy, I wished him no ill, and I do believe we're better off for his having been here.

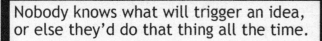

Nobody knows what will trigger an idea, or else they'd do that thing all the time.

I think the two best birthdays are when you turn sixteen, and twenty-one.

First you get to drive, then you get to drink.

Yes, that's when all the pieces fall into place.

The key is to recognize a good idea when you get one and then build on it, rather than dismissing it out of hand.

People'd look forward to their birthdays if they got a new legal right every ten years.

You'd start small. You turn thirty, U-turns are legal.

At forty, you get to slander your parents, because if you still want to at that age, they've probably earned it.

While building on the idea, try to steer it in a productive direction if you can.

What new right would you get when you turn fifty?

Recreational marijuana use.

I didn't know you smoked pot.

I never touch the stuff. I just know a few fifty-year-olds who could stand to mellow out.

Don't be over-critical. You'll have more success trying to make things work than looking for reasons they can't.

When you turn one hundred, you can murder, as long as you do it unassisted with your bare hands, and the victim is under thirty.

HA! YES! Good luck getting away, junior! You can't make U-turns!!

basicinstructions.net

BASIC INSTRUCTIONS

How to Impress NOBODY

by Scott MEYER

Nothing is less impressive than obviously trying to impress people. Here are a few popular and transparent ways people try.

How are you?

Impressive.

Impressively what?

Why don't you tell me?

You really don't want me to.

Being a know-it-all: Flaunting your knowledge tells people that you think they're stupid. Nobody likes that.

I don't like chickens.

THAT'S STUPID! CHICKENS ARE GREAT! You just haven't ever been around chickens.

I grew up on a farm. We had chickens. I hated them.

You had the wrong kind of chickens.

Yes. The live, uncooked kind.

Owning something cool: An object can be impressive. Owning it proves nothing, not even that you really could afford it.

This is my chicken. She's the best!

NGAAAAH!! How'd you get it here that fast?!

She was just out in the car.

You carry your chicken around with you in your car?

You would too if you had a chicken this good.

Jerking people around: Fun is fun, but making others unhappy for your pleasure does not make you seem funny or clever.

Will you put that thing away?!

Eventually, when you stop cringing in that amusing way.

Or when your arm gets tired.

Nah, I can switch arms. You can't switch personalities.

© 2011: Scott Meyer

basicinstructions.net

It's probably because I grew up on a farm, but the idea of suburbanites raising chickens for pleasure is beyond me. It'd be like using an outhouse recreationally. The whole reason we created civilization was to not have to do this stuff. That's what makes it civilized.

BASIC INSTRUCTIONS

How to Ruin the Story You Are Telling

by Scott MEYER

The fastest way to ruin a story is to oversell it, creating expectations in your listeners' minds the story can't fulfill.

Emphasizing parts of a story tells your listener what's important. Emphasizing everything tells them none of it is.

You can be the protagonist of your story, but you shouldn't be the hero. A story about your awesomeness is just bragging.

A story should end with the point, like a joke ends with the punchline. Not knowing the point makes this impossible.

basicinstructions.net

138

BASIC INSTRUCTIONS — How to Discuss Video Games — by Scott MEYER

First of all, only discuss video games with someone who is interested in them.

I've always said video games are a waste of money.

Well, Mom, we don't all have the foresight to invest our money the way you did, in ultra-slim cigarettes and country music cassettes.

When discussing games with someone, start by asking what system they use.

I have an Xbox 360.

I have a PS3, so I look down on you, and will continue to until I buy a 360 as a second console.

By which time, I'll have bought a PS3.

What a glorious day that will be.

If someone's into games you don't like, be nice about it and try not to judge.

I have a wii!

Dude, everybody has a wii. Most of us have the good taste not to talk about it.

That's why they named it after going to the bathroom.

Keep the conversation positive. Focus on games you like and why you like them.

When I was a teenager, I liked beat-'em-ups. Then I moved on to shooters. Now I mostly play strategy games.

I gravitate toward games that give me what I'm looking for in real life.

Control.

Nope. Detachment and plausible deniability.

basicinstructions.net

 Okay, I gotta admit, the first panel of this one is pretty mean. Not so mean that I'm not going to include it in this book, but mean enough to make me feel bad as I include it in this book.

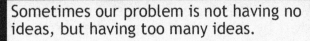

Sometimes our problem is not having no ideas, but having too many ideas.

Heat, pressure, and time. The three things that make a diamond also make a waffle.

I think you've used that in a comic before.

Hmmmm. "How to Re-use an Idea."

I think you've done that before too.

Look at the possibilities and see if one option leaps out, either as best or worst.

I don't know who coined the term "Hershey Squirts," but I bet they worked for Nestle.

Try something else.

"Hershey Squirts" sounds like a promotional cartoon about kids who love chocolate.

Something that doesn't involve "Hershey Squirts."

That rules out half of my ideas.

If you are indecisive, the opinion of a second party can often be helpful.

Winnie the Pooh and Fozzie the Bear. Both bears. Same color. Brothers? I bet they can't stand each other.

What do you think?

I think your idea file is like Rorschach's journal, if Rorschach was an idiot.

You can wallow in indecision forever, but there comes a point where you have to just pick one option and go with it.

I'm either going to do a comic about "Hershey Squirts," or one about Strunk and White using their knowledge of grammar and usage to solve crimes.

The grammar sticklers in your comments section should enjoy that.

Yes. "Hershey Squirts" it is.

© 2011: Scott Meyer

basicinstructions.net

BASIC INSTRUCTIONS

How to Summarize a Complex Topic

by Scott MEYER

There are many topics that people know are important, but find too complex.

I've been reading about mutual funds.

I know nothing about those.

It's not all that complicated. You see, there...

Yeah, I didn't learn nothing about mutual funds because I find them so fascinating.

Start by describing the topic in the broadest, simplest terms you can.

There are index funds that do whatever the market does, and managed funds, where experts try to beat the market.

So you're either betting on the unthinking market or human experts.

Yup.

I think my money'd be on the unthinking market.

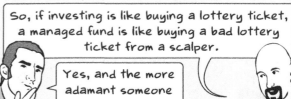

And you'd only be right about 80% of the time.

Carefully choose which details you add. The goal is to inform but not confuse.

So index funds usually do better than managed funds.

Yes, because funds charge fees, and some charge more than others.

Let me guess. Managed funds charge more fees.

Managers don't pay for themselves.

Truer words were never spoken.

End by summing up the topic, preferably in one short, memorable sentence.

So, if investing is like buying a lottery ticket, a managed fund is like buying a bad lottery ticket from a scalper.

Yes, and the more adamant someone is that they know what's best, the more suspicious you should be.

Are you sure?

Eh, pretty sure.

All right then.

basicinstructions.net

This was written pretty much on a dare from a reader, one David Rothschild. The challenge was to take a dry, complex topic and boil it down into something interesting, entertaining and easily understood. I'm proud of the final result, and will never take such a dare again.

Misunderstandings are common, but many of them can be easily avoided.

Don't mince words. Express yourself as clearly, directly, and politely as possible.

Choosing the right word can go a long way toward making yourself understood.

Be descriptive. Use words and imagery to make people feel the way you feel.

© 2011: Scott Meyer

basicinstructions.net

142

BASIC INSTRUCTIONS
How to Figure Out "Who's That For?!"
by Scott MEYER
It's the oldest trick in the observational comedy book. Find something that seems to have no purpose and ask who uses it.
Did I.T. figure out what was wrong with your computer?
I don't wanna talk about it.
Had you hit the Number Lock button again?
Don't be silly! It was the Insert button.
Really, who are those buttons for? They should both be labelled "sabotage."
If you genuinely want to know who uses a seemingly useless item, first determine what it actually does.
The Number Lock has a use. If you turn it off, you can use the number pad to move your cursor around a document.
That is useful.
I'll write myself a note to remind myself of that.
Shall I put the note ON MY MOUSE, OR NEXT TO THE ARROW KEYS??
Once you know what the item does, ask yourself who would find it useful.
Some people don't like using mice.
HORRIBLE LUDDITES!
Would a Luddite really be using a computer?
A horrible one would.
Try not to be intolerant. Remember, there are probably items you use that others have little use for.
Another key that does more harm than good is the Caps Lock.
Nonsense!
But ... you are always accidentally writing entire e-mails with the Caps Lock on!
iT'S NO ACCIDENT. i LOVE cAPS lOCK. iT'S LIKE pIG lATIN FOR YOUR FINGERS!
© 2011: Scott Meyer
basicinstructions.net

Having friends and family from out of town come to visit you is stressful, but it is also well worth the stress.

I can't wait for your visit! It's gonna be great!

It's good to hear that. You never come to visit us.

Yeah. I didn't move away from our hometown as soon as I turned eighteen because I liked it there.

When planning their visit, start with practical issues, like where they'll stay.

I've reserved a room at a great little hotel near where I live.

That's okay. I had hoped we could stay at your place.

That's no problem.

I'll be staying at this great little hotel near where I live.

You want your guests to be entertained. Put careful thought into what they'll do.

I'm gonna take you to see all the big tourist attractions.

I'm sure you've seen all that stuff a million times.

Not at all! We locals avoid all those places 'cause they're always crawling with tourists.

I figure I'll already have tourists with me, so what the hell?

The hardest part is often the logistics: getting from where they are staying to what they are doing.

Don't worry about getting a car. I'm happy to drive you around.

Well, I insist on paying for your gas.

Splendid. The first tourist attraction on our list is the world's most expensive gas station.

basicinstructions.net

BASIC INSTRUCTIONS — How to Make a Crass Generalization

by Scott MEYER

Panel 1:

Loudly spouting crass generalizations makes you look like a fool. You have to ease into your crass generalizations.

The Kingdome was the manliest building ever built.

Didn't people say it looked like an old hubcap sitting on a rusty rim?

Nothing manlier than that!

Didn't they blow it up?

Yes. It even died manly.

Panel 2:

Try to be interesting or entertaining. People need a reason to listen to things with which they are inclined to disagree.

And the men's rooms at the Kingdome were designed entirely for men, entirely by men.

You'd think they'd be a virtual paradise for men.

A Phal-halla, if you will.

I combined Valhalla and phallus.

Yeah, I get it.

You didn't laugh.

That's how you know I got it.

Panel 3:

As you zero in on your point, be clear. Make sure nobody will misunderstand.

The Kingdome's men's rooms had concrete floors and cinderblock walls. There were two metal troughs. One had a urinal cake in it, the other had a soap dispenser on the wall next to it.

EEEWWWWW! What happened if you got the wrong trough?!

First there'd be yelling, then there'd be laughing.

Panel 4:

When you state the crass generalization, make it clear that there are exceptions, but the rule holds true.

Men, in general, will trade dignity for efficiency.

That explains their taste in clothes.

And humor And cars. And movies. And women.

My goal was to help you understand men, not respect them.

basicinstructions.net

The Kingdome men's rooms were exactly as described here. They always seemed to me to have been designed for livestock. I'm pretty sure they cleaned up after every game with high pressure hoses and harsh chemicals. Again, manly.

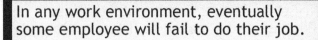

Panel 1: In any work environment, eventually some employee will fail to do their job.

"Jenkins isn't filling out his RJ-17 form."

"As the leader, it's my job to make sure everyone does their job."

"Let me guess. My job is to go confront Jenkins for you."

"Yup. Now get to work."

Panel 2: First, avoid misunderstandings by making sure that they know what their job is.

"You're expected to fill out the RJ-17 form."

"Really?"

"Okay, expected isn't the right word. More like "repeatedly told." I expect you to ignore me."

"And I aim to exceed your expectations."

Panel 3: Try to make them understand why their task is so vital to the organization.

"Look, it's your job!"

"Yeah, then what's your job?"

"Apparently to repeatedly tell you to do your job!"

"If I do my job, you'll have nothing to do."

"You say that like it's a bad thing."

Panel 4: If someone won't do their job, it's time for the person in charge to do theirs.

"I told him to do his job. He refused. The ball is in your court."

"Tell him I said that was unacceptable."

"That's your answer? Sending me to talk to him again?"

"You said the ball's in my court."

"Yeah, so what?"

"You're the ball."

basicinstructions.net

We all need help sometimes, often from the very last person we'd want to ask.

Rocket Hat, I've had you attacked, captured and brought here against your will so I could ask for your assistance.

I'm not good at asking for help.

It doesn't show, Sire.

Explain the situation so that the person you're asking knows your need is real.

We Moon-Men are at war with the inhabitants of Saturn's utterly insignificant moon, Titan.

It's barely 50% larger than our moon! Yet they have the gall to resent us for calling our moon "The Moon."

We got the domain name first. Those are the breaks!

Make it clear that you aren't happy to ask for help, but that you'll both benefit.

Rocket Hat, I know we have our differences.

For instance, the Emperor hasn't made friends with the Titanians like you have.

SILENCE!

And you don't want you dead, like the Emperor does.

THE DETAILS ARE UNIMPORTANT!

Once you've asked, back off. They'll decide whether they will help you or not.

I can't believe he stood by while I got savagely beaten. He didn't move a muscle or say a word.

It's so out of character for him.

You didn't help me either.

Yes! I have the virtue of consistency.

basicinstructions.net

Since this comic is about help, I'm going to take this opportunity to thank the publishers of my first three books: Dark Horse Books and Don't Eat Any Bugs Productions. I also want to thank Missy, Ric, and everybody else who has supported Basic Instructions over the years.

Dignified Hedonism
A collection of Basic Instructions
Volume 4 by Scott Meyer

Written, drawn,
and designed by
Scott Meyer

Rocket Hat Industries
P.O. Box 692191
Orlando, FL 32869-2191

ISBN-10:0615889530

ISBN-13: 978-0615889535

Made in the USA
Coppell, TX
12 March 2021